Fo

Church Buildings and their co
as a beautiful historical treasu
past. But what is far less stud
find in the graveyards surrounding the Church
characteristic of every society is how they buried and
remembered their dead. And during the 18th Century many of the
memorials to the departed express so much individuality,
creativity, artistry and meaning, which can be a joy to study,
understand and appreciate.

At Elsdon we find one of the best preserved and complete
collections of 18th Century Gravestones in England. These stones
tell us much about the lives, hopes, fears and faith of the people
who lived in the Parish some 300 years ago, and the exquisite
skills of the Stonemasons who designed and created these stones.
Allow yourself the time to look closely at these stones and unlock
the meaning of the symbols carved onto them. And don't be
uncomfortable doing so. These stones were created to be looked
at, understood and appreciated. They are messages from the
dead to the living. They speak of the faith of the dead and their
fervent hope for resurrection. They remind the living that life is
short and uncertain and that they will one day be judged on their
behaviours and beliefs. The stones were placed so that
Parishioners attending Church, or participating in the range of
social and commercial activities that commonly took place in
Churchyards, couldn't fail to read them. And they were
designed so that even the illiterate could understand the
messages written on the stones, as they are presented in symbolic
as well as narrative forms.

Peter Ryder has written this book to help visitors find, understand and appreciate some of the finest 18th Century stones in the Elsdon Churchyard. To unlock the meaning of the symbols used and the messages they convey. Allow the stones to stimulate your imagination and curiosity. To think about the people buried here, the people who created these stones and the society in which they lived. These stones are still speaking to us, this book will help you understand their language and unlock their meaning.

Mark Hatton

Plan by Keith Maddison, used with permission

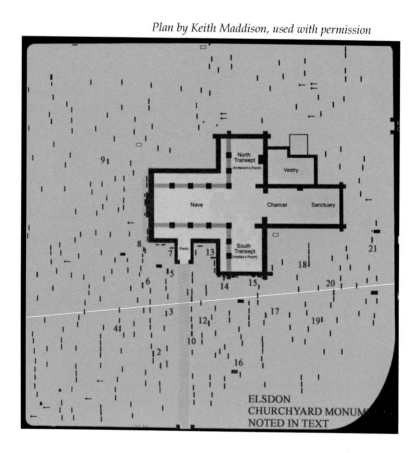

ELSDON
CHURCHYARD MONUM
NOTED IN TEXT

Everything we leave behind is a memorial to our human lives, either communally or individually. An old church like St Cuthbert's is a communal monument to a body of people meeting for worship; there may have been a few important individuals who contributed towards the growth of the building, but their names are now lost to us. However, within and all around the church stand smaller monuments raised to commemorate specific human individuals, indicating their places of burial and telling us something of both their individual lives, and the beliefs and tastes of society as it was at that time. This little book concentrates on the particularly attractive and distinctive collection of 18th century gravestones in Elsdon churchyard. It is not an academic treatise (although there is certainly scope for one to be written) but a celebration of the folk art that they demonstrate, and the light that they shed on the very different culture of the 1700s. Elsdon has a number of older monuments as well, as well of course as more recent ones, and these will be briefly mentioned, but the focus of this work is on the 18th century headstones, and in particular about twenty of the best examples, which really are worth looking at in detail…

Inside the Church

Our oldest grave stone of all, sometimes called 'The Elsdon Stone' (right), really has nothing to do with the church. Its form – an upright slab with an arched top – is classically that of a headstone, but it is Roman and came from High Rochester (12 km to the north-west), where it probably stood alongside Dere Street, the Roman road, outside the fort – such was the customary Roman place of burial. It has little art about it, only

words, but seems to be unique in the country in setting out the entire military career of a Roman officer – his name is gone, but we are told the stone was set up by his wife Julia Lucilla.

Cross Shaft, St Cuthbert's Church, Elsdon
built into internal west jamb of south door

drawn PFR 1 4 2019

0   30 cm

As far as we know there is nothing Roman actually in Elsdon, but there has been a church here for a long time. Traditionally, the dedication to St Cuthbert marks it as a resting place of the saint's coffin when it was being carried around the North of England by monks fleeing from the Vikings, in the 870s, but there is tentative evidence that there was already a church here (it would have been an obvious place for them to come to). It could have been a small monastery; just one stone survives to provide evidence for it, part of what was perhaps a cross shaft (now built into the internal west jamb of the south doorway) with traces of vine-scroll sculpture (left) showing affinities with 8th or 9th century stones at Simonburn and Rothbury, both probable monastic sites at the time, with Elsdon on the road midway between them.

In the Middle Ages, a troubled time here in Northumberland, the churchyard would have looked quite different to today. The people who could afford permanent monuments – and there may not have been that many – would have been buried under recumbent stone slabs usually marked with a cross, sometimes with a smaller upstanding cross at head and foot. Left without a monument it seems were the hundreds of men buried in a common pit under the north aisle, whose bones were found in the 1870s, and are thought have been victims of the 1386 Battle of Otterburn.

Medieval cross-slabs re-used as lintels over the south doorway

Medieval monuments hardly ever remain in situ. The landowning families would have had their burials inside the church, in chapels in which masses were said for their souls. In the later medieval period they might aspire to stone effigies, or to brass-inlaid slabs.

Then came the great storm of the Reformation, when the whole world of the church, its ceremonies and imagery changed, and the Church of England quit the Church of Rome. We have little evidence of what churchyards looked like in the 1500s and early 1600s. The use of the cross as an emblem passed out of fashion; such medieval slabs as we have today usually owe their survival to pragmatic re-use as a lintel or window sill, to be disinterred from the church building by Victorian restorers. There are a dozen or so in St Cuthbert's Church[1].

(right) A simple cross slab, perhaps of the 12th century, in the south transept

---

[1] They are described in detail in the book 'A Tale of Three Churches'....

William Brown memorial on North Tranept pier

Before leaving the church and looking at the predominantly 18th century stones in the churchyard, it is worth taking a look at one wall monument, on the west side of the arch into the north transept, to William Brown of Ravenscleugh (d1741), because it gives us an introduction to some of the symbolism seen on the headstones (p7). It is a splendid and high-quality piece of work, which even retains much of its original colouring. At the head of the inscribed panel (flanked by grieving cherubs) is a bearded head, which can be presumed to be at least an attempt at a portrait of the 67-year old William, set directly above a skull or death's head – a reference to his mortal remains, buried 'nigh this place' as the inscription tells us - whilst directly above is a winged head, an attempt at a slightly-younger version of the countenance below (and still very serious-looking) which represents his spirit taking flight. It is these death's heads and winged spirits, emblems of mortality and immortality, that characterise so many of the 18th century headstones in Elsdon and other Northumberland churchyards. These and other emblems, some grisly to modern eyes, demonstrate both the accepted transcience of life, and the hope of Resurrection.

So where does all this folk art come from? As already said, there seems a more or less complete discontinuity between it and anything medieval. We have very little in the way of graveyard monuments between the Reformation and the Civil War. A lot of the mortality emblems characteristic of Elsdon and other Northumberland church yards may link to the even more exuberant tradition of sepulchral art that was developing North of the Border, where in particular emblems denoting trades etc (which were present on medieval slabs) are more common than in England.

In the Churchyard

(1) Entering the churchyard from the south, 10 m up the path on the left is a very striking stone which straightaway confronts the modern viewer with the different tastes and susceptibilities of the 18ᵗʰ century as regards to death and the permissible imagery associated with it. It is the back of the stone one sees – whereas the fronts of headstones conventionally face east, this one must have been turned round, so that its gruesome reverse today welcomes visitors. What it shows is a hanging bag or fold of cloth, slung between two rings, and containing a jumble of bones, with a central human skull just above them; sitting on top of the skull is a winged hourglass.

A memorable composition carved in bold relief, colloquially the 'Bag of Bones' stone. The other side of the stone has a sunk panel, which presumably contained an inscription, which a combination of weathering and lichen have completely erased, with above it a human head with feathered wings, sometimes termed a 'cherub' but more fittingly seen as the spirit of the departed winging their ways upwards to Heaven – hence 'a winged spirit'.

The two prime emblems here are this winged spirit and the death's head, the reminder of grim mortality, and they are almost always found on opposite sides of the stone. Inside the church the 1741 wall monument to William Brown of Ravenscleugh is topped by a human head (William himself?) with a skull directly below and ascending spirit directly above…. Winged spirits are ubiquitous on 18ᵗʰ century stones, even more so than death's heads. The hourglass – sometimes winged ('time flies…'), sometimes not - is another obvious symbol of mortality.

'The Bag of Bones'

(2) A couple of metres north-west of the 'Bag of Bones' is a taller stone to Hannah, wife of William Ord, who died in 1754. One wonders if this is its real date, as directly below is an inscription, in identical lettering, to her grandson Ralph Ord, d 1828 – and then a third, in quite different script, to Isabel Ord d. 1877. The

shaped top has an attractive winged spirit – but the reverse is a bit of a shock, a very neatly cut shaped panel with a death's head, hourglass and a mighty pair of crossed bones. Whatever the date of the stone, the imagery looks mid-18th century but the very professional quality of the carving feels more of the early 19th century. There are very similar stones, probably the work of the same mason, at Hartburn.

Adam and Eve: The Fall

(3) A few metres further up the path, and again on the left, is a small stone with a triangular gabled top just a little wider than the stone beneath, and the remains of an inscription. 'Here lies… Katharin.. ..died…' which is really not sufficiently informative. But this is another stone where the value is in the reverse, on which we have a high-relief carving, not of the conventional mortality emblems, but of a charmingly naive Garden of Eden scene with the central tree heavy with fruit and leaves, with Adam on the left and Eve (being approached by the snake) on the right. This is by far the most common Scriptural scene to appear on headstones; it is especially common north of the Border[2]. Contrast these stones with medieval grave slabs, which almost always show a cross, often elaborated in to a Tree-like form, but this is the Tree of Life form, as a symbol of Redemption. Here it is the Tree of the Knowledge of Good and Evil, and the symbolism is a cautionary one, of the Fall rather than subsequent Salvation. In the long backlash of the Reformation the cross, although today again accepted as a universal Christian motif, is completely absent, through its association with what would have then been termed Popery.

[2] Wilsher, Betty (1992) Adam and Eve scenes on kirkyard monuments in the Scottish Lowlands. Proceeding of the Society of Antiquaries of Scotland 122, 413-51

(4) In the third row of headstones back from the path, and just a little south of (3) is a rather square headstone with a shaped top, and an inscription 'This is the Burial Place of Joseph Corbett...' , a reminder of the fact that a person could purchase a burial plot for their own kith and kin – a walk round any old churchyard will show clusters of monuments to members of the same family. The inscription here is not all legible, but Margaret his daughter and Harriet his wife are mentioned, and her date of death seems to be '1784'. The top of the stone resembles an open swan-neck pediment in form, and has a panel, carved in relief, with a central death's head carried on a winged hourglass, with to the r. Father Time's scythe and to the l. a circular object that proves on close inspection to be a serpent swallowing its own tail. This is quite a common symbol, sometimes known as 'Ouroborous' that symbolises eternity, but one can have a field day speculating as to its origins – present in ancient Egyptian iconography, and in Greek magical tradition, it has links with Alchemy and Gnosticism as well, although it is perhaps doubtful that 18th-century Elsdon was a hotbed of either of these.

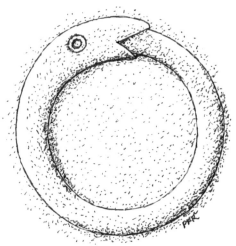

(5) On the left of the path close to the church porch is a small headstone that has a neatly-shaped segmental-arched top springing from volutes carried by Ionic pilasters (stones (7) and (21) are virtually identical in form). The front has a winged spirit above an inscription 'The Burial Place/ of Andrew Turnbu..'. The mason has made a fundamental setting-out error, coming up against the raised border at this point, and has to slot in a single small 'l' above. So this is Andrew Turnbull's burial place, not his grave – it is Walter his son who was buried here – the date is worn but may be '1735'. Once again it is the reverse that is the delight, with a raised figure of Father Time, winged and bearded, with a scythe in his l. hand and a dart in his r., pointing down onto a

skull; on his l. alongside the scythe is a long upright bone, and there are other minor motifs difficult to identify. Above his head is the incised text 'MEMENTO MORI' – 'Remember Death', which seems a bit unnecessary given the power of the motifs.

Father Time

(6) A few metres south-west of (5), and in the third row of stones back from the path, is a stone to Thomas Hedley, d.1762. It has a simple shaped top and a winged spirit of conventional form, but the reverse is really interesting ; it has a death's head and crossed bones, but not proudly placed centrally as in Hannah Ord's stone (2) but low down, almost at ground level, almost as if they were just showing through the earth. Was this the sculptor's intention?

Just above the turf....

(7)   On the west side of the church porch, re-set relatively recently, to face south, a headstone with a worn inscription to 'Jane Alb...', with a date that may be '1750'. In form it is very similar to stones (5) and (21); it is the reverse that is of interest, as it bears a superimposed pair of winged spirits, the upper with wings aloft, the lower with wings folded. Their significance remains a mystery; as far as one can see the inscription commemorates a single individual.

8) Close to the south-west corner of the south aisle of the church a broken headstone is propped up alongside others. Little remains visible on the front – other than the date '1791' at the very bottom, which is almost certainly a secondary addition, but the back of the stone has had another figure of Father Time, this time in the act of sweeping his scythe, standing on a pair of crossed bones.

Passing the west end of the church, note various stones propped against it, which include two stone coffins. These are almost certainly medieval, used for high-status burials, and were probably topped with cross-slab grave covers, several examples of which survive inside the church. They may have been found in the churchyard, or possibly under the church floor.

(9) About 8 m west of the north-west corner of the church is a headstone to James White which is a very conventional Victorian stone (1844), that would be outside the scope of those included here, except for one thing, the first line of its inscription 'LET NO MAN MOVE THESE BONES' which must hark back to one of the great scares of the early 19th century, the 'Resurrectionist' threat of the digging up of recent burials to

provide cadavers for medieval schools, which proved a lucrative trade. Such concerns are particularly evident in the churchyards of Lowland Scotland where mortsafes (metal cages laid over a burial) and watch houses commonly occur; in Northumberland there are watch houses at Doddington and Belford. The 1832 Anatomy Act (which allowed the 'anatomists' to be supplied with corpses of the poor from workhouses) greatly reduced this dubious trade, but clearly its memory was still fresh in 1844, even in a remote village like Elsdon.

(10) Returning to the path from the main gate to the church, on the east c 15 m from the gate is a small headstone, the first of a row of five . The inscription is hard to read, but the surname appears to be 'Dobson' (there is a later Dobson headstone alongside) and the date '1756'. Carved in relief on the shaped top, within a border of curving leaves, are a slightly different suite of emblems. In the centre is a raised hand holding an open book, with on the l. an hourglass, and on the r. what is probably a trumpet – both probably images from the Book of Revelation, the Book of Life (chapter 21, 27 - 'nothing impure shall enter Heaven, only those who have their names written in the Lamb's Book of Life') and the one of the seven trumpets (chapter 6, 8-12) sounded by angels to usher in the final judgements.

(11) Four stones north of (9), alongside the path, is a sizeable and well-preserved stone, 'the burial place of William and Ann Hall'. Ann died in 1807; the final part of the inscription, recording the death of William in 1856, is clearly added by a different mason. What is interesting is the general style of the stone, moving on from the cruder and more vernacular patterns of the mid-18th century. The whole stone has a well-carved border of leaf ornament, and it takes the popular swan-neck pediment like form, like the twenty-year older Corbett headstone (4) – except that now, instead of its central death's head, there is just a roundel with a petalled flower. Grim mortality emblems are absent - the only one of the traditional motifs to survive is the winged spirit, hardly the most cheerful-looking of the species, between two anthemion leaves and sundry lobed leaves and spiral volutes.

(12) 2 m to the north-east of (10) is another well-preserved stone of much the same date, to Jane and James Hedley of Greenchesters'; she died in 1805 and he in 1809, along with their son 'who died in infancy'. The imagery shows the same development; the rather charming conjoined winged spirit has two faces – presumably representing Jane and James, with on either side what look like rather stylised representations of trumpets, and flowers.

(13) Against the west side of the south transept is a very interesting small headstone, now set facing south – this is almost certainly not its original position, but a recent re-positioning so that both sides of it can be examined. Its top is a variant on the swan-neck pediment, but with two piercings on either side of a central motif that may be intended to be a stylised face, although hardly a very elegant one; it seems to have foliage issuing in the 'green man' tradition. Below is a neatly- incised italic inscription to Mabel Ridley; the date is lost. The reverse of the stone is better

preserved, and most interesting. There is a very fine winged spirit, but below it on the left a tree with a sheep below it, and on the r. a figure kneeling at an altar with another standing upright behind, about to strike it with a knife or sword. There can be no doubt about the Bible story depicted here; it is from Genesis 22, when Abraham is commanded to sacrifice his son Isaac, but when he is about to do so his hand is stayed, and a ram, caught in a nearby thicket, is substituted. A recent study of Scottish headstones[3] cites this as the second most popular Bible Story to figure, with about 10 examples (after 54 of Adam and Eve)

---

[3] Brown, Hamish (2008) A Scottish Graveyard Miscellany, Birlinn, 99

The Sacrifice of Isaac (note ram, on l. caught in thicket)

(14) Is another headstone that has probably been re-set, this time the right way round, against the south wall of the aisle of the south transept. It is quite a small stone with a simply shaped stepped ogee top and an inscription to 'Isbel' wife of 'Eduard' Hedlie, who died in 1722; early in the 18th century, it is quite a rustic vernacular piece. On the back, carved in very bold relief, is a big death's head (seen side on rather than with the more usually hollow-eyed frontal stare) above crossed bones, with beneath them a recumbent hourglass. Above are the incised words 'MEMENTO MORI'. The spacing of the lettering suggests that the mason did not possess a high degree of literacy….

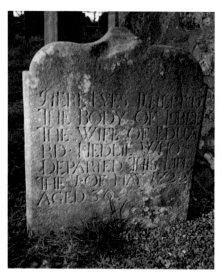

(15) A little further east against the south end of the transept is another obviously-reset stone, altogether a little more sophisticated. It has a swept segmental top, with a moulded label, above a neatly-cut inscription to Ephraim Hall, who died in 1791. Rising damp has caused the lower half of the face to decay into illegibility, leaving the top in pristine condition. The emblems, at the top, are a self-swallowing serpent and an hourglass, mortality emblems but now a more esoteric than the more brutal memento mori of the headstones of the previous generation.

(16) Returning to the south side of the churchyard, and a monument c 10m north-east of the gate, this is not a headstone but a table tomb, a recumbent slab standing on six moulded legs, of convex section, bordered with an intermittent roll moulding that has an undeniable resemblance to the pastry crust of a pie.... At the west end of the slab is a cherub, upside down in relation to the neatly-incised inscription to Isabel, wife of Edward Laing. The date is no longer legible, but there are some close stylistic similarities to the excellent wall monument inside the church to William Brown of Ravencleugh, d.1741, which we have already seen.

(17)   About 8 m south of the south-east corner of the South Transept is a headstone to William Hedley of Otterburn, who died in 1787 at the age of 69, and it is included here to demonstrate the change in character of the headstones in the last decades of the 18th century. There is regular geometrical ornament – two raised roundels with spiral ribs, and a line of raised saltire crosses between, beneath a panel flanked by spiral volutes, with in its centre an upright motif that could be a broken pillar or a snuffed-out candle. Below the inscription, in a different font, is a continuation commemorating Margaret Hedley, Williams's granddaughter, who over century later, died in 1892, at the age of 104. Do your sums; there is both longevity and late child-bearing here one would not expect.

(18) The southernmost of a north-south row of four close-set headstones due south of the chancel, a headstone with an inscription to Dorothy, wife of …. Hall. The date is illegible. Above is a cherub, and on the reverse a death's-head resting on an hourglass, above a big pair of crossed bones. The design seems identical to the stone to Hannah Ord (no3) , which is dated 1754; it is presumably carved by the same mason, and must be around the same date.

(19) About 15 m south of the chancel, and just a little to the east of the row containing (17), a headstone to Anne, wife of Robert Bighel, who died 1718/9 – an example of the 'double dates' used in the earlier 18th century, relating to the legal year actually beginning on March 25 and the calendar year on January 1st. Anne, dying on March 3rd, then died in the legal year 1718 and the calendar year 1719; all this resolved in 1750 when Britain formally took on the Gregorian Julian calendar.

The reverse is quite similar to (18), except that the crossed bones are directly below the death's head, and below them is an hourglass with precisely the same sort of wings as cherubs usually have, ie with the hourglass placed exactly as if it were a cherub's head.

(20) Three stones to the south-west of (19) is a headstone with a shaped segmental top; on the east is a big winged spirit and an inscription (now heavily lichened) 'The Burial Place of John Brown' with a date that may be '1711'. On the reverse is a high-relief death's head above crossed bones.

((21) About 5 m east of the south-east corner of the chancel is a small headstone, in form very like (5) and (7) with a shaped segmental-arched top springing from volutes carried by Ionic pilasters. The inscription is partly legible: 'The Burial Place of… Bail….Curate of El/sdon…. 1771.' A Jeremiah Baile or Bailes is recorded as curate at 'Elsden' in 1728-1746[4] ; the '1771' visible at the base of the stone is probably part of a secondary inscription. On the reverse of the stone is a relief-carved coat of arms, which is very similar, but not identical, to a published Bailes family crest[5].

[4]https://theclergydatabase.org.uk/jsp/persons/CreatePersonFrames.jsp?PersonID=135348

[5] https://www.thetreemaker.com/family-crest-b/bailes/england.html

And afterwards....

Of course, the graveyard continues in use, and the majority of the four hundred or so monuments are from the last two centuries, and just like their 18th-century predecessors they demonstrate the continuing change of style and taste, and the choice of motifs that we think appropriate to commemorate our dead. Rather than be

carved by a local mason (or family of masons) by the mid-19th century you were more liable to order from a copy-book, and so designs begin to be replicated, not just locally but country-wide. Here is a typical example from Elsdon, a mid-Victorian angel, now in a revived medieval style, pointing to a scroll on which the name of the deceased is seen as being written....

New American Library
Published by New American Library, a division of
Penguin Group (USA) Inc., 375 Hudson Street,
New York, New York 10014, U.S.A.
Penguin Books Ltd, 80 Strand,
London WC2R 0RL, England
Penguin Books Australia Ltd, 250 Camberwell Road,
Camberwell, Victoria 3124, Australia
Penguin Books Canada Ltd, 10 Alcorn Avenue,
Toronto, Ontario, Canada M4V 3B2
Penguin Books (N.Z.) Ltd, Cnr Rosedale and Airborne Roads,
Albany, Auckland 1310, New Zealand

Penguin Books Ltd, Registered Offices:
80 Strand, London WC2R 0RL, England

First published by New American Library,
a division of Penguin Group (USA) Inc.

First Printing, January 2004
10 9 8 7 6 5 4 3 2 1

 REGISTERED TRADEMARK—MARCA REGISTRADA

LIBRARY OF CONGRESS CATALOGING-IN-PUBLICATION DATA
Jacobs, David.
   The shield : notes from the barn : the elite strike team files / by David Jacobs.
      p. cm.
      ISBN 0-451-21167-7
   1. Shield (Television program) I. Title.
PN1992.77.S476J33   2004
791.45'72—dc22   2003020303

Printed in the United States of America

PUBLISHER'S NOTE
This is a work of fiction. Names, characters, places, and incidents either are the product of the author's imagination or are used fictitiously, and any resemblance to actual persons, living or dead, business establishments, events, or locales is entirely coincidental.

BOOKS ARE AVAILABLE AT QUANTITY DISCOUNTS WHEN USED TO PROMOTE PRODUCTS OR SERVICES. FOR INFORMATION PLEASE WRITE TO PREMIUM MARKETING DIVISION, PENGUIN GROUP (USA) INC., 375 HUDSON STREET, NEW YORK, NEW YORK 10014.

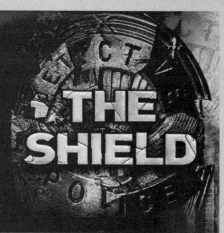

NOTES FROM THE BARN:
The Elite Strike Team Files

David Jacobs

New American Library

FOREWORD

I was navigating my 1997 Dodge Neon through a driving rainstorm from the *Angel* offices in Santa Monica to the FX building in West Los Angeles. What should have been a twenty-minute ride had turned into an hour-long, gridlocked ordeal. I had given myself extra time to make the trip, but I'd used it all up about ten minutes earlier. I was going to be late. Which meant the meeting would run late. Which meant I'd be late getting home to dinner with Cathy and our daughter, Haley, who had just turned one a couple weeks earlier. I was wet, tired, and grumpy and had no idea my life was about to be turned upside down.

It was November 2000, and it was already pitch-black outside when I pulled into the parking structure. I had been told that FX was possibly interested in making a pilot I had written called "The Barn". I knew it was an extreme long shot. I was a young writer, with barely three years of work experience in television, who had written a script filled with profanity, nudity, and violence in which the "hero" of the piece commits a heinous, unforgivable act at the end of the episode. Not a reliable recipe for success.

I was meeting with Kevin Reilly, the President of Entertainment, who had enjoyed great success at NBC and then Brillstein-Grey. We spent the first few minutes exchanging pleasantries and then he dropped the bombshell. FX wanted to make my pilot, but only if I would executive produce it. I told Kevin later that I thought he was crazy for making the offer, and to this day he's never given me a more satisfying explanation than he "had a feeling." As thrilled as I was, I had heard far too many tales of the Hollywood system to feel comfortable. I waited for it all to go to hell.

First, I had my heart set on hiring Scott Brazil to produce the pilot and help guide me creatively. He had an amazing track record and an infectious affinity for the script. He seemed to like it more than I did. FX and Fox Television Studios said yes. Together, Scott and I settled on Clark Johnson as the director we wanted. He had never directed a pilot, but the work he had done was amazing and he was on the same wavelength as Scott and I about the material. FX, FTVS, and Sony Pictures Television said yes.

I figured the trouble would begin at the casting process. We wanted Michael Chiklis, of *The Commish* fame, to play Vic. The actor they remembered from that role wasn't right for Vic. The actor that walked in to audition for them had shaved his head, slimmed down, and bulked up. FX said yes. We wanted CCH Pounder to play a role that had been written for a man, though she was decidedly a woman. FX said yes. For the other roles, we wanted wonderful actors who weren't exactly the most recognizable faces around. Actors who seemed believable, authentic. FX said yes to all of them.

When it came time to make the pilot, we waited for the network to try to roughen up the edges of the script. They never asked. After the pilot was made, we assumed they wouldn't have the courage to pick us up. They did. We assumed they would do an amateurish job of marketing the show. They did it brilliantly. When it came time for the premiere of what was now called *The Shield*, we worried that people wouldn't watch. They did.

It's a Herculean task to produce a television show every seven business days. Scripts have to be written, locations have to be scouted, directors have to be prepped, sets have to be built, props have to be made, costumes have to be made, actors have to prepare, scenes have to be shot under difficult conditions and extraordinary time pressures, episodes have to be edited, music has to be found, sound has to be mixed, and a network and, in our case, two studios have to be kept updated on the status of every one of these endeavors. It's an impossible job that our producers, writers, cast, crew, and postproduction staff make possible thirteen times a year.

If you're reading this, there's a good chance you're one of our incredibly loyal fans. On behalf of everyone who works on the show, thank you for watching. Without you, *The Shield* would be just a script I shoved into a drawer and forgot about long ago.

SHAWN RYAN
October 31, 2003

C hairman Mao once famously observed, "Political power comes out of the barrel of a gun."

In today's Los Angeles, California, it may justly be said, "Political power comes out of the barrel of a police officer's gun."

Los Angeles's policing situation has its own unique problems. Currently, L.A. has about seven thousand police officers. By comparison, New York City has some forty thousand officers. L.A. voters don't like paying taxes to build a police infrastructure. Therefore, the department has to do more with less.

Historically, this has created an approach to law enforcement that is proactive and results-oriented. Departmental officers have a reputation for being aggressive against active and potential lawbreakers. They come down hard on criminals. They make up in vigor and initiative what they lack in numbers.

In L.A., the war on crime is not mere phrasemaking, but an official policy and credo. This is a city that contains more than fifty thousand gang members, most of them well armed.

The public demands results of its police department. When crime is down and the public feels safe, all is well. When crime goes up and the public feels unsafe, they turn up the heat on police and politicians.

If it gets hot enough, it can burn the powerful right out of their prestigious posts.

Down on the Farm

In recent years, few problems have proved as potentially volatile as those arising in the city's high-crime Farmington district—known locally as the Farm.

The establishment of the Farmington police division seems to have created as many problems as it was supposed to have solved.

In less than two years, the district has seen drug gang wars, serial killers, mass murders, riots, the ambush killings of police officers, and a heroin epidemic in the schools.

And that's just from the criminal side of the ledger.

The Farmington police force itself has been accused of being dysfunctional. Its elite antigang unit, the Strike Team, under the aggressive leadership of Detective Vic Mackey, has been accused of brutality, corruption, drug theft, and even murder. Like the precinct, the squad was the creation of Ben Gilroy, former assistant chief of police, who later experienced a dramatic and very public fall from grace.

At the height of the scandals, the previous chief of police was removed from his post.

The New Chief

Which brings us to his successor, the new chief of police, Tommy Aaron Bankston.

Political insiders rank him as a man who knows where the bodies are buried and won't hesitate to use that knowledge to protect his position against threats both actual and potential.

One of the ways he maintains his power is through the use of the Special Investigations Unit (SIU), his own personal intelligence service.

The SIU is a team of investigators who are attached to the chief's office. It's not so much a detective squad as an intelligence-collecting unit. Its members do not gather information on criminal activities in anticipation of future prosecution—they collect information that might be useful to the chief at some future date.

Information on the underworld and the overworld, on mobsters, politicians, businesspersons, Hollywood celebrities, community activists, government offi-

cials—anyone who has or might have some real or possible involvement with the department in general and Chief Bankston in particular.

SIU membership is selective and highly secretive. Its files are kept in an annex to the chief's office, with entrance restricted to Bankston and a handful of his most trusted aides. Call it blackmail material, or call it leverage. By any name, it translates to power gained and kept.

The Special Investigations Unit's CONFIDENTIAL REPORT ON THE FARMINGTON DIVISION—hereafter to be referred to as the Confidential Report.

Bankston's predecessor lost his job primarily because of his own greed and corruption. The Farmington scandals were the last straw in a series of setbacks, culminating in his dismissal. Chief Bankston is known to be a man who doesn't like surprises. One of his first acts on taking office was to order the SIU to launch a wide-ranging probe into the tortuous history of the Farmington Division precinct, with a special focus on the activities of Vic Mackey's Strike Team.

The result of that investigation is the report that follows.

ALL PROPERTY SUBJECT TO POLICE INSPECTION TEAM

POLICE CODE 4033 A

Strictly Confidential

Its very title says CONFIDENTIAL REPORT. Why, then, are you reading it?

Because someone or several someones in the SIU, or very high up in Chief Bankston's staff, thought that it would be a good idea to make this report public for internal political reasons. Perhaps whoever leaked the report wanted to embarrass Bankston or the department or both. Or maybe he or she or they thought its contents were something the public ought to know. Copies of this report were clandestinely passed to receptive parties in the L.A. media, who bannered it in the headlines and led off with it during the nightly news.

At first, department spokespersons refused to comment on the report. When it wouldn't go away, they then branded it as a hoax or a forgery.

After extensive fact-checking procedures by independent law enforcement experts and document analysts verified the authenticity of this document, the department officially returned to its stance of "No comment."

However, it's known that a "furious" Chief Bankston immediately ordered an investigation to determine who leaked the material.

That investigation has so far come up empty-handed.

Mindful of the public's right to know, and of the important issues of law and order, crime and punishment, and justice and injustice addressed by its stark depiction of the gritty realities besetting the men and women of an urban police precinct, the publisher has made available this special edition of the complete CONFIDENTIAL REPORT ON THE FARMINGTON DIVISION.

No matter what your feelings may be about cops, whether pro or con, after reading the twisted tale of life and times down on the Farm, you may find yourself agreeing with the sentiment expressed in the old song by Gilbert and Sullivan: "A policeman's lot is not a happy one."

1. OVERVIEW

REPORT ON THE FARMINGTON DIVISION

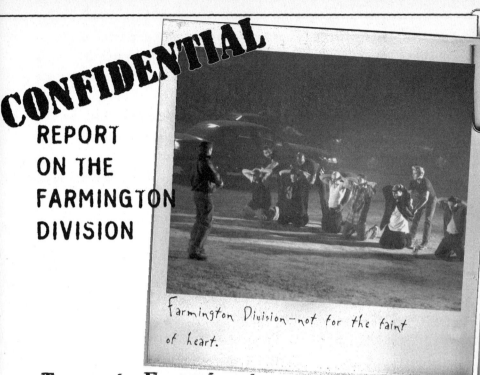

Farmington Division—not for the faint of heart.

Target: Farmington

Farmington Division stands on the front lines of the department's war on crime. As in other combat zones, it's a dangerous place of loose alliances, heavy firepower, and sharp, sudden reversals of fate.

Established about two years ago, the division has been in the headlines ever since. It's a place where reputations are made—and lost.

Crime can't be eliminated, but it can be contained and controlled. Farmington is where the police containment vessel is closest to coming apart.

In the last twenty-four months, the district has seen the ambush murders of three police officers and the critical wounding of a fourth; two days of rioting (the so-called Two Days of Blood); a heroin epidemic reaching into the schools; gang wars; mass murders; and the arrest (for corruption and vehicular manslaughter) of one of L.A.'s most powerful police officials, Assistant Chief Benjamin Gilroy.

We note here that Gilroy was a creation of the previous chief of police.

This SIU unit was charged with making a thorough investigation of the Farmington Division police precinct, from its formation two years ago through the present day.

The epicenter of precinct shock waves has been the Strike Team, an elite antigang, antidrug unit that has been accused (and cleared) of drug theft, brutality, corruption, and even murder.

All of these charges have come to nothing. But as the saying goes, where there's smoke . . .

History and Background

Farmington is a low-income, high-population-density, high-crime area that has been described as a war zone.

The district is 83 percent African-American and Latino, with a plurality of the latter. The majority of the citizens are honest, hardworking, law-abiding individuals. However, they live under the shadow of a pervasive and violent criminal element.

The area is a crazy-quilt patchwork of "turf" claimed by various street gangs, of which the most powerful are the black One-Niners, Monks, Jack-uzis, and Compton Crowns, and the Latino gangs Los Magnificos ("Los Mags") and the Toros.

Farmington (or the Farm) has one of the city's highest murder rates, of which the lead cause is gang violence, followed by drug killings. Burglaries, car thefts, armed robberies, and muggings are daily occurrences. Many street corners are thronged with drug dealers and street hustlers, and male and female prostitutes.

Responding to the troubled area's high crime rate, Assistant Chief Ben Gilroy established an experimental police precinct where none had existed before, the Farmington Division. Personnel were recruited from other divisions.

Infrastructure of sorts existed in the form of an abandoned church, which was retrofitted to serve as a station house. It was equipped with holding cells, interrogation rooms, a briefing room, a squad room, administrative offices, an armory, evidence lockers, etc.

Early on, the officers tagged the large, cavernous structure as "the Barn," a nickname that stuck.

The division's mandate was clear. It had to produce results, fast. Otherwise, the experiment would be judged a failure, and the precinct would most likely be closed and its personnel reassigned.

Positive results were defined as noticeable drops in the crime statistics.

Strike Team

At the heart of Gilroy's conception for the division was the creation of a Strike Team, a small, mobile, elite unit targeting drug and gang activities.

The team was authorized by the previous chief

IAD Surveillance Photo: #42A. Subject: Det. Mackey excessive-force complaints.

of police. Funding for it came out of the chief's administrative budget, disbursed by Gilroy.

Gilroy chose Detective Vic Mackey as his Strike Team leader. The rest of the squad consisted of three other detectives: Shane Vendrell, Curtis Lemansky, and Ronnie Gardocki.

Within the first few days of their working together, the team made an important arrest, busting a gang leader for a drive-by shooting and dealing crack cocaine.

The squad has since racked up an impressive record. In the last two years it has broken a number of major cases, including the Women's Shelter Massacre, the Cherrypoppers vice operation specializing in underage teen girls, the Gun Club Massacre, and the Jenny Reborg abduction.

It was instrumental in taking down Armando and Navaro Quintero, Mexican mobsters who sought to unify all the Farm's Latino gangs into one supergang. This was done at great personal risk, with one team member being tortured and the entire squad being marked for death.

The team nabbed dangerous fugitive Dante Fell from under the noses of the federal authorities, who'd been unsuccessfully pursuing him for years.

It played a vital role in apprehending the 911 ambush-murder cop killers. More recently, when the resurgent Johnnies street gang began murdering citizens at random, the squad took the gang executioners off the street before they coud kill more.

At the same time, from the start, Mackey's squad has been dogged by civilian complaints alleging brutality, corruption, and even outright criminality.

In this they are not alone. Farmington Division police (uniformed patrol officers and detectives) have one of the city's highest levels of excessive-force complaints. Its reputation for violent policing has given rise to the street nickname "the harm on the Farm."

The number of complaints has been dropping significantly while the crime

rate has slowed down since the precinct first opened and the Strike Team went into business.

Unfortunately, these complaints, substantiated or not, have reached the press. Newspapers and TV stations have been quick to highlight some of the more sensational allegations involving the Barn.

Downside

While the Strike Team is at the heart of the most sensational charges, the rest of the division has seen more than its share of woes, highlights (or lowlights) of which include:

- A Strike Team member shot and killed in the line of duty.
- Allegations of Strike Team corruption and drug theft, with the attendant bad press accompanying such charges.
- The 911 emergency call delay murders of two women, leading to the subsequent ambush killings of police and forty-eight hours of rioting in the community.
- The Gilroy affair.
- Kingpin Armando "Armadillo" Quintero's drug mob targeting the district.
- The release of the Kellis report, putting Captain Aceveda and the Strike Team at the center of the division's problems.

Lawsuits, brutality complaints, IAD investigations, police scandals and street riots put the precinct in the limelight. The district's sensational level of nonstop criminality keeps it there.

The Barn and Strike Team have created a lot of headaches for the department.

They've also caught a lot of crooks and saved a lot of lives.

Our investigation focused on six individuals who've played major roles in the life and times of Farmington Division. They are:

- **Detective Vic Mackey, the hard-charging head of the Strike Team.**
- **Captain David Aceveda, the precinct's commanding officer.**
- **Detective Claudette Wyms, held by some to be the moral center of the division.**
- **Detective Holland "Dutch" Wagenbach, Wyms's partner, an erratic but brilliant sleuth.**
- **Officer Danielle "Danny" Sofer, a veteran uniformed street cop.**
- **Officer Julien Lowe, a rookie patrolman and Sofer's partner.**

Attention must also be paid to Ben Gilroy, the founder of the Barn and Strike Team, who crossed the line and was destroyed by his own creation.

2. DETECTIVE VIC MACKEY: THE HAMMER

IAD Surveillance Photo: #42D.
Subject: Det. Mackey excessive-
force complaints.

Surveillance Transcript: 081-33102 Location ref:
FARM-4510

Vic Mackey: Good cop and bad cop have left for the
day. I'm a different kind of cop.

Detective Vic Mackey is a courageous, dedicated police officer who has been decorated with the department's highest medal for valor.

Detective Mackey is a crooked cop, a killer who may have murdered a brother officer.

Mackey is a devoted family man, a loving husband and father.

Mackey is a womanizer and adulterer whose marriage is headed for the divorce courts.

The Strike Team is the division's most effective antigang, antidrug squad, responsible for 50 percent of the precinct's arrests.

The Strike Team controls the Farm's drug trade, protecting favored dealers from arrest and busting their competitors.

Which of the above statements are true? None, some, or all?

This investigation was charged with determining the true state of affairs in the Farmington Division. On the Farm, the Strike Team is at the center of the action. From day one, it's been a major player in the key events of the precinct's history. Its purported scandals have gotten the worst press, while its successes have generated the most positive headlines.

For the purposes of the Office of the Chief of Police, the Strike Team is a double-edged sword. It can cut both ways, for good or ill. Handled properly, it can be a tremendous asset, both in crushing crime and in creating favorable publicity. Mishandled, it could create a mushrooming scandal with the potential to impact the very highest levels of the department (i.e., this office) and the city government.

Meet Vic Mackey

Integral to the squad's dynamics is the personality of team leader Vic Mackey.

The son of a bricklayer, Mackey has been a member of the department for fifteen years. He was a uniformed street cop before getting his gold detective's shield.

Two years ago, when Farmington Division was being formed, Mackey's career in the department had essentially stalled. His record was mixed. He rated top marks for bravery, leadership, and work ethic. Both as a uniformed patrolman and as a plainclothes detective, he'd earned numerous commendations and citations for heroism in the line of duty. His list of major busts was impressive.

On the downside, the record was marked by complaints of excessive force and questionable police procedures. He was not regarded as one who'd let legal technicalities get in the way of making an arrest.

More damaging for Mackey, however, was his record of run-ins with established

Farmington File Photo: Farm. apartment bust. Case #12-A.

authority. He'd feuded frequently with supervisors and superior officers. His record showed black marks for insubordination and failure to follow orders he disagreed with.

In short, Mackey had earned a reputation as a maverick. Not the sort of label that helps one rise to the upper levels of the department.

One person in Mackey's corner, however, was his career-long friend and mentor, Assistant Chief Ben Gilroy. Vital to Gilroy's conception of Farmington Division was a precinct Strike Team. Such teams had already proven their worth in achieving major drops in crime in relatively short periods of time.

Mackey wanted to head the Farm Strike Team. Wanted it and needed it. It was his ticket out of career limbo.

Others didn't want him to have it. He'd made enemies among departmental higher-ups, powerful enemies.

Mackey put it to Gilroy on a personal basis, asking him as a favor to try to swing the post his way. Gilroy had the clout to get what he wanted, and he wanted Mackey as team leader. Mackey got the post.

Mackey had worked well in the past with Detective Shane Vendrell and picked him for the team. Vendrell brought in Detectives Curtis Lemansky and Ronald Gardocki. The latter two had worked with Vendrell before, but not with Mackey.

The unit was complete.

First Strike

It was perhaps inevitable that two such strong personalities as Captain David Aceveda and Detective Vic Mackey would take an instant dislike to each other. Both were driven, ambitious, and strong-willed. Adding to the antagonism was the built-in adversarial divide between cool technocratic administrator and aggressive street cop.

Aceveda was the division's commanding officer and Mackey's superior. But Mackey's pull with Assistant Chief Gilroy ensured that he would have a court of appeal to protest any Aceveda dictate he didn't like.

Mainly, though, for whatever reason of personal chemistry, Aceveda and Mackey just plain didn't like each other.

In itself, this is not uncommon. Every rookie in the department knows that an officer doesn't have to like someone to work with him—or for him.

As will be seen, one thing that Aceveda and Mackey have in common is that they are both survivors. At times when both their careers were in jeopardy, they managed to form an alliance long enough to handle their mutual enemy before resuming their private war.

Farmington Division came into being because Gilroy had promised it would deliver quick results in cutting district crime. From day one, the pressure was on for the Barn to produce. The clock was ticking. Those who'd opposed its creation were waiting for the chance to pronounce it a failure.

The Strike Team needed a big win, fast. That would buy it time and breathing space from hostile headquarters brass and Aceveda.

The four individuals in the unit had to work as a team right out of the starting gate. They had to coalesce, come together.

They hit the ground running.

Surveillance Transcript: 035-86381 Location ref:
FARM-6620

Mackey (to Strike Team): Trust isn't something that
happens overnight, and trust me, where we're going,
we're going to need it.

But undercover operations don't happen overnight. They need time to build trust with the targeted individual or group, to put an operative on the inside, and to set up a bust that'll go down hassle-free and hold up in court.

The team didn't have that time. They needed a shortcut.

A drug dealer with delusions of grandeur, Lionel Phipps was trying to expand into the protection racket by shaking down, among others, the local street hookers.

Ringo the pimp refused to pay. Soon after, a drive-by shooter chopped one of his stable, a hustler named Rhonda.

The Strike Team busted Rondell Robinson, a member of Phipps's crew, on a narcotics charge. Mackey hustled Robinson into Aceveda's office. Robinson wanted to deal. In return for immunity, he'd give up Phipps. A big fish being a better catch than a medium-sized fish, Aceveda okayed the deal.

Robinson then signed a statement saying that he had recently delivered crack cocaine to Phipps. A warrant was obtained and Phipps's residence was raided by the Strike Team and backup. Also present was Aceveda, who'd told Mackey, "I want to see how you work."

It was a uniformed member of the backup team, rookie officer Julien Lowe, who actually found the drugs, which were hidden in the bathroom. Phipps indignantly denied that the drugs were his, saying that they'd been planted.

He was then confronted with a set of Tec-9 machine pistols, also found on the premises. The weapons were later identified by Ballistics as having been the ones used in the hooker drive-by shooting.

The Strike Team had made its first big bust—a solid one.

It bought them some time.

Home Life

A man's private life often informs his public and professional life. Vic Mackey's family includes his wife, Corrine, and their three children: daughter Cassidy, eight; son Matthew, five; and baby girl Megan.

The Mackeys own a suburban home complete with backyard barbecue and below-ground pool; several personal vehicles; and a boat. Every year, the family takes a two-week vacation trip to a lakeside resort. Their standard of living and financial assets are outwardly little different from those of the families of other officers of Mackey's pay grade.

Matthew Mackey has been diagnosed as having autism. He was enrolled as a student at Glen Ridge, a special-needs private school for autistic children. Tuition is a stiff $25,000 per year. A heavy expense, especially on an honest cop's salary.

Mackey's finances have been closely vetted on more than one occasion: by IAD investigators during the drug theft probe, and by Barn detective

Claudette Wyms during the Quintero drug wars.

In both cases, Mackey came up clean—no evidence of financial impropriety or assets beyond his means were found.

However, now that Vic and Corrine Mackey seem headed for divorce court, the picture may change. Lots of things come out in divorce court.

Subject: Det. Mackey excessive-force complaints.

Surveillance Transcript: 323-76007 Location ref: FARM-0182

Gilroy: You've gotta spend more time with your family, Vic. You lose them before you know it.

In the Line of Duty

For the next fourteen months after start-up, the Strike Team kept on doing its thing, hammering drug dealers and street gangs and racking up an outstanding felony arrest record, solid busts that held up in court and led to convictions. The team had earned an enviable reputation on the street. It was respected and feared.

Farmington crime statistics dropped noticeably, generating positive press.

The mayor was happy, the D.A. was happy, and most important, headquarters's top brass were happy.

The drop in crime stats saw a corresponding increase in complaints of excessive force and police brutality. But when the complainants are career criminals, the complaints are easily ignored.

After all, the thinking goes, once they've been busted, what else are they going to say? Alleged violation of their rights may be their only hope of escaping a prison term.

A measure of the team's effectiveness is that, during a routine street sweep, several dozen persons wanted on open warrants voluntarily surrendered themselves at the Barn. Queried by the desk sergeant, one of them explained, "Vic Mackey called. Told me to turn myself in."

A fifth member was added to the squad. Detective Terry Crowley, a veteran officer with a fine record, transferred over from Robbery Division to join the Farm team. For his first few months, Crowley mostly served as driver, not taking part in any team raids.

Tragically, while participating in his first raid as a full-fledged Strike Team member, Crowley was killed in the line of duty, shot dead by drug dealer Two-Time.

Mackey and Vendrell then shot and killed Two-Time.

As with all cases in which an officer is slain, an IAD investigation followed. It found that Detective Crowley had been killed in the line of duty, that standard operating procedure had been followed, and that the team had proceeded properly. No reprimands were issued.

Following close on the heels of Crowley's death came the accusation that Mackey and Vendrell had stolen two bricks of cocaine during a drug bust. The accuser, Officer Julien Lowe, had been present at the bust.

The charge prompted an IAD investigation, which was soon short-circuited by Lowe's retraction of his original accusation.

Not before damage had been done. The charges and IAD probe, which were both supposed to be confidential, were leaked to the press, which had a field day running front-page features about the subject.

When the probe was dropped, and its subjects cleared, the story was shunted from page one and buried on the back pages—thus associating the Strike Team (and by extension the division) with the taint of corruption.

Belief that Barn higher-ups were protecting favored drug dealers was the rationale offered by Nation of Islam (NOI) mosque leader Xavier Salaam for his group's peaceful occupation of the police station.

The occupation ended with the finding of the body of Rondell Robinson, the dealer who'd been harassing the NOI mosque.

Robinson, who'd given up Lionel Phipps, was a registered Confidential Informant (CI) of Vic Mackey's.

Call 911 and Die

The Grove is a predominantly black neighborhood in the district. Two local residents, Tonya Ann Cramer and Violet Roosevelt, both black, were slain by Wally Forton, the white boyfriend of Cramer's daughter.

The victims and concerned neighbors had put in a number of 911 emergency calls for help almost an hour before police arrived. By then, it was too late. The women were dead and the killer long gone.

It was revealed that, after Tonya Cramer had first called 911, Forton left the apartment and milled around outside. Twenty minutes later, with police still absent from the scene, he went back in, escalating the confrontation from shouts to violence, murder, and mutilation.

News about the fatal delay incensed the community, putting it in a state of

unrest. Angry crowds protested in the streets. A majority of them were made up of young men. Many of them were gang members.

Lawful protests erupted into rioting and looting, unleashing what came to be known as the Two Days of Blood.

Worse was yet to come.

Teenage Twanya had been raised by the two dead women. Since police negligence had led to their deaths, she would revenge herself by randomly shooting police officers dead. Who they were didn't matter, as long as they were cops.

She roped two teen male friends of hers, Sonny and Benji, into the plan, unleashing the 911 ambush killings. With crude irony, they phoned in a fake 911 call, luring a police patrol car to a lonely site. Hiding in ambush, the shooters opened fire on the defenseless cops, killing one and critically wounding another.

The next day, they struck again, this time killing both officers and stealing the badges from their dead bodies.

The situation started to improve when Captain Aceveda and Detective Claudette Wyms led a squad that apprehended Wally Forton. Still, there were three cop killers on the loose.

The first break in the case came when Mackey and Vendrell, acting on a tip, apprehended Sonny, one of the shooters. From him, they learned the hiding place of the other two.

(Sonny later claimed that he'd been tortured into revealing the information.)

Mackey's Strike Team, accompanied by Aceveda and backup units, entered an abandoned building given up to squatters. That was where Twanya and Benji were hiding. Twanya was killed while resisting arrest; Benji was taken alive.

With shrewd media savvy, Aceveda arranged to have the press on hand at the Barn when he brought in the 911 shooters.

It gave his ongoing candidacy in the upcoming city council primary a big boost. Boosted the Strike Team, the division, and the department, too.

The Gilroy Factor

Aceveda and Mackey had to overcome their differences to work together. The unifying factor was Assistant Chief Gilroy.

Gilroy had tried to hang the fatal 911 manpower shortage on Aceveda, even though it was Gilroy himself who'd diverted police patrol units from the Grove to other neighborhoods, leaving it underpoliced, with only two units to cover it.

Gilroy had further undercut Aceveda by setting up a command post in the Barn and taking command of operations, shunting the captain off to one side.

Mackey had his own reasons for locking horns with Gilroy—reasons that were revealed when Mackey brought Gilroy into the Barn under arrest and in handcuffs.

Gilroy had committed vehicular manslaughter, hitting Anthony Nunez, seventeen, with his car and fleeing the scene of the accident. (A witness to the scene, the victim's friend, was later found dead in what was classed as a gang killing.)

The accident was only the tip of the iceberg. Present in the death car with the married Gilroy was Sedona Tellez, his girlfriend and partner in an intricate real estate fraud scheme.

The plan involved diverting police away from the Grove, thus triggering a crime wave, which would lower property values in the neighborhood. Using an offshore front company, the plotters would buy up the properties at bargain prices. Gilroy would then increase police presence in the Grove, stifling crime and causing a rise in property values. The properties would be sold at a hefty profit to developers.

But the scheme came apart after the hit-and-run. Detective Dutch Wagenbach found Tellez, and Aceveda convinced her to testify.

There is no need here to rehash the public relations nightmare generated by the Gilroy arrest. But every villain engenders a hero, it seems.

In this case, the hero was Aceveda, whose handling of the riot and the apprehension of the 911 shooters and Gilroy made him a press darling and a figure of public acclaim overnight.

Needless to say, his newfound celebrity status made him few friends among headquarters brass. On principle, cops don't like to see other cops getting famous busting cops.

If Aceveda was worried by that, he didn't show it.

Family Ties

Shock waves from the Gilroy affair sent serious disruptions into Mackey's home life. It seemed to begin with a curious incident.

The record shows that, during the hit-and-run investigation, the Los Angeles Sheriff's Office received an emergency phone call from Mackey. He said that his wife had reported a prowler around the house and that he was on his way home.

An LASO substation was located near the Mackey house. Several patrol cars and deputies arrived at the locale. There was apparently some confusion, with Corrine Mackey professing bewilderment at why the deputies were there.

Mackey soon arrived, assuring the deputies that everything was under control. A deputy later recalled overhearing Corrine Mackey telling her husband that Ben Gilroy had been there, keeping a dinner engagement that Vic Mackey must have forgotten. (Gilroy was already gone when the deputies arrived.)

In hindsight, the obvious conclusion was that Mackey feared that Gilroy might do harm to his family.

There being nothing else for them to do, the deputies left.

Mackey hurriedly hustled his wife and children out of the house. All they had were a few hastily packed suitcases. He put them up in a motel. Staying

with them, presumably as a bodyguard, was Strike Team detective Curtis Lemansky.

Following Gilroy's arrest, Corrine Mackey and the children returned to the family home. They were there only long enough to pack their things and depart.

Mackey came home to a deserted house. A recorded phone message from Corrine begged him not to look for them if he still loved her.

She needed to get away, she said, to think about what had happened, what her marriage had become, what to do next.

Soon after, Mackey hired a private investigator to find his wife and kids.

Five weeks passed. The absence of Mackey's family put him under a lot of stress. His work suffered accordingly. He was moody, preoccupied—didn't have his head in the game. Relations with other Strike Team members declined, with Mackey becoming curt, short-tempered, quarrelsome.

An informant told Mackey the location of a storehouse of stolen goods being operated by a fence named Fleetwood Walker. Going there to investigate, Mackey came across a gun deal in progress.

One of Fleetwood's crew, Quint, pulled a gun. Mackey shot him in the leg. Fleetwood took advantage of the distraction and shot Mackey in the side. Mackey shot Quint dead, while Fleetwood escaped. He was caught later.

Mackey was hospitalized with gunshot wounds. During this period, he achieved a reconciliation of sorts with Corrine, who with the kids moved back into the Mackey house. Released from the hospital, Mackey continued his recovery at home.

While laid up, he busied himself by devising a new spin on the Toys for Guns program. The program encouraged local residents to turn in guns, no questions asked, trading them for children's toys. A way to get guns off the street.

Mackey's twist was to tie the exchange in with a phony "lottery" sting. Those turning in guns were eligible to participate in a big-prize lottery to be conducted by the department. All they had to do was fill out a free lottery ticket, listing their names and addresses.

If any of the guns were found to be linked to past crimes, their unsuspecting owners could be easily traced thanks to the information they'd submitted.

Mackey was examined by a departmental physician, who found him fit to return to duty.

On his first day back on the job, a ceremony was held at the station, awarding him the department's highest honor, the medal for valor and courage under fire. Presenting the award to him was Captain Aceveda.

Ironically, Mackey had been recommended for the honor by Lanie Kellis, a civilian auditor appointed by the city council to investigate the division in light of the recent riots, killings, and the Gilroy debacle.

It was ironic because Kellis would later become Mackey's nemesis, going to extraordinary lengths to try to nail him for the precinct corruption she came to believe he was responsible for.

That same day, Mackey busted Armenian-American mobster Alex Eznik.

Coming home, he was confronted by Corrine. She reminded him that she'd agreed to let him live in their home only while his wounds were healing. Now that he was fit for work, she asked him to leave the family residence.

He packed his bags and moved into a room at the Farmington Residence Suites, a location conveniently close to the Barn. While relatively clean and crime-free, the building was somewhat shabby and down-market. Mackey was overheard remarking to another officer that his new home was not a place he would feel comfortable taking his children to.

Armadillo Wars

The next challenge for the division was the Quintero drug wars. At the forefront of that deadly conflict were Mackey and the Strike Team. They risked all, with some paying a heavy price.

Armando "Armadillo" Quintero and his brother, Navaro, were Mexican drug mobsters who sought to establish a stronghold in the United States. With fifteen federal warrants hanging over his head, Navaro had to stay south of the border. He anchored one end of the gang's drug pipeline in Tijuana.

Armadillo was the advance man in the north. He decided that the pipeline's other end would be in Farmington, where he planned to unite all the Latino street gangs into one supergang.

Armadillo began by using trusted Mexican compadres. Major members of such gangs as the Toros and Los Mags were "invited" to join his operation. Those who refused were ruthlessly eliminated by being burned to death, as a warning to others.

As his distribution organization took shape, he destabilized the competition by indirectly supplying them with poison-laced drug shipments. One of those so supplied was drug dealer Tio, who'd replaced Rondell Robinson as the district's black drug kingpin.

It was inevitable that Mackey and Armadillo would soon cross paths.

Mackey struck first, apprehending Navaro Quintero. Navaro claimed that Mackey and the Strike Team had gone into Mexico, abducted him at gunpoint, taken a $400,000 ransom for his safe return but refused to release him, and then smuggled him back across the border, drugged and in a car trunk.

All of which would have been patently illegal, if true. But Navaro had no proof. He went to jail.

Consolidating his plans for conquest, Armadillo executed Tio and several of his lieutenants, gruesomely burning them to death.

It was at this time that Detective Claudette Wyms became suspicious of Mackey's actions in the case. She gained possession of Tio's ledger, which recorded monthly payments to an individual identified only as "Landlord." Wyms suspected that Tio had been paying off someone higher up the ladder. Was Vic Mackey "Landlord"?

Aceveda authorized a warrant allowing Wyms to examine Mackey's bank deposits and other financial statements. She compared several deposits in Mackey's bank accounts with payments made by Tio to Landlord, but was unable to find a correlation between the two.

Financially, Mackey had come up clean.

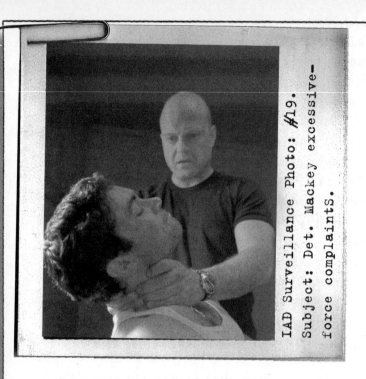

IAD Surveillance Photo: #19.
Subject: Det. Mackey excessive—
force complaints.

Project Greenlight

Armadillo next began flooding Farmington schools with heroin, targeting not only high schools but also junior high schools and even grade schools. His dealers first gave away free samples, producing a wave of drug overdoses and deaths among the youngsters.

Unable to find Armadillo, Mackey tried to reach him through his brother, Navaro Quintero. Contacting Navaro in jail, Mackey told him to tell Armadillo to stop pushing heroin to schoolkids. Otherwise, Mackey would have Navaro "greenlit."

Greenlighting is jailhouse slang for arranging to have someone in prison killed.

Mackey later said that of course he was only bluffing, that he really wouldn't have had Navaro killed.

In any case, Navaro was convinced enough of Mackey's sincerity to communicate the threat to Armadillo. Not one to be easily intimidated, Armadillo countered by himself having Navaro greenlit.

While making a phone call, Navaro was stabbed to death by another inmate, as yet unidentified.

Armadillo then turned the tables on Mackey and the rest of the Strike Team. Each member of the squad was under sentence of death, with bounties posted on their heads by the gang leader.

Fearing for his family, Mackey had a $2,000 alarm system installed in the house. He did not explain his reasons for doing this to Corrine Mackey. Unknown to her, he'd also hired private detective Gordie Liman to have the Mackey kids covered by his operatives while they were at school.

Someone tried to break into the house. Luckily, it happened when no one was home.

The crisis came to a head when Strike Team detective Ronnie Gardocki was attacked by Armadillo's gang. He was viciously beaten and tortured by having his face held to the coiled burner of an electric stove.

Gardocki was hospitalized in the intensive care unit. Eventually he recovered and returned to full active duty. Extensive skin grafts helped repair the damage to his face.

The rest of the squad tracked Armadillo to his hideout. Before they could take him, he phoned the police, offering to surrender to them. Patrol units arrived and took him into custody. He was handcuffed and transported to the holding cell in the station.

Intriguingly, Armadillo's face bore burn marks nearly identical to Gardocki's, although the drug lord's injuries had been inflicted two months earlier.

Armadillo remained silent, except to insist on speaking with Mackey alone. The two met in an interrogation room. What they talked about is a matter for conjecture since, before the conversation began, Mackey switched off the closed-circuit video camera monitoring the cell, cutting off outside communication.

Emerging a few minutes later, Mackey said merely that Quintero had refused to talk and demanded to see his lawyer.

Quintero was incarcerated in the station's holding cell, sharing the space with several other prisoners. One of them was Pinto, an aging Los Mags member who'd been arrested on a drug violation by Officer Danny Sofer. As the arresting officer, she was charged with the responsibility of searching Pinto before he was placed in the cage, as the holding cell is called.

Mackey wasn't laughing after his wife had him arrested.

Somehow, though, Pinto managed to smuggle a knife inside. He attacked Armadillo, stabbing him nine times and killing him. Subsequently, Danny Sofer maintained that she'd searched Pinto thoroughly and found no such weapon on his person and that he must have gotten it elsewhere, perhaps from another prisoner in the cage.

Investigation later showed that Pinto and Armadillo were former drug business associates. Pinto said that he'd been shoved aside by the other's Mexican-born clique and relegated to the lowly role of a glorified errand boy.

By killing Armadillo, he felt he'd regained his status and street credibility, certifying him as a man of power in the criminal world.

He'd rather be a respected killer in prison than a free nonentity out on the street.

So ended the matter of the Quintero brothers.

The Split

Mackey served his wife with divorce papers. It was a preemptive strike, one urged on him by a high-powered divorce lawyer he'd met through private eye Gordie Liman.

Going to his motel room to confront him, Corrine Mackey caught her husband with another woman.

Later at the family house, Mackey made the unhappy discovery that his key no longer opened the doors. The locks had been changed. Seeing Matthew running about untended, Mackey broke in.

Technically, he was in violation of a restraining order that Corrine had earlier sworn out against him. LASO deputies came to the Barn to arrest Mackey, leading him away in handcuffs. He spent a night in the county jail.

As primary election day neared, someone broke into Lanie Kellis's office at the Barn and stole a copy of her report on the division, leaking it to the newspapers. The report located the center of what she termed the questionable operations of the Strike Team, enabled by an unholy alliance between Mackey and Aceveda.

Countering some of the bad press was the Strike Team's capture that same day of top wanted fugitive Dante Fell.

At that point, the future of the Strike Team and its leader, Vic Mackey, was very much in doubt.

3. THE SQUAD

Farmington File Photo: Strike Team.

The Strike Team's group dynamic: Mackey is the leader, Shane Vendrell is the enforcer, Curtis Lemansky is the anchor, and Ronnie Gardocki is the technical specialist.

Shane Vendrell

Vendrell is originally from somewhere in the vicinity of Atlanta, Georgia. He's quick-tempered, fast with a fist or a gun. He's a womanizer whose dangerous liaisons have gotten him into trouble more than once.

He's also incredibly loyal to Vic Mackey.

Having worked well together in the past, he and Mackey knew they were on the same wavelength. Vendrell was Mackey's first choice for the Strike Team.

Dude, Where's My Car?

In the matter of alleged drug thefts during the Armenian mob's Ara's Pastry shop drug bust, Officer Julien Lowe stated that he'd seen Vic Mackey steal two bricks of cocaine and place them in Shane Vendrell's weapons bag, which Vendrell carried out of the building.

The day after the big bust, the desk sergeant on duty at the Barn logged a phone call from a woman complaining that, the night before, her teenage son and his friend had been "terrorized" by a man claiming to be a police officer.

They'd been riding around in her SUV, a late-model blue Navigator, when a car pulled up alongside them. In it was a man in civilian clothes waving a gun, ordering them to pull over. They obeyed, coming to a halt in front of Robin's Food Market.

Forcing them out of the vehicle at gunpoint, the man accused them of stealing the Navigator and ordered them to lie facedown on the asphalt while he searched the SUV. Whatever he was looking for, he didn't find it.

Apparently realizing that he'd made a mistake, he got back into his car and drove away. One of the youths got the car's license plate number, which when checked was revealed to belong to a female acquaintance of Detective Shane Vendrell.

Questioned by Captain Aceveda, Vendrell stated that, the night before, a departmental vehicle issued to him, a 2002 blue Navigator SUV, had been stolen while parked at curbside. He'd been seeking to recover it.

Aceveda put out an All-Points Bulletin (APB) on the vehicle. It was recovered that afternoon by Officers Sofer and Lowe and was searched on-site by Aceveda himself. The search did not turn up anything.

Subsequently, Deena, the car thief, stated that after stealing the vehicle she'd found two bricks of cocaine concealed in it. She said she'd passed the drugs to her boyfriend. He was found dead in his apartment, the victim of a cerebral aneurysm brought about by snorting lethally potent cocaine.

No bricks of cocaine were found on the premises.

Officer Lowe's subsequent retraction of his statement brought the IAD probe into Mackey and Vendrell's alleged drug theft to a close.

Gun Club

Around this time, Vendrell's relationship with Mackey hit some rough patches. Mackey thought Vendrell was slipping and let him know it. He threatened to drop him from the team.

Worsening the situation was an incident in which Vendrell noticed a book about autism in Mackey's car. Not knowing the facts, he made some crude remarks about "retards" that steamed Mackey good.

That was when Mackey first threatened to cut him from the team.

During the Gun Club Massacre investigation, Vendrell redeemed himself in Mackey's eyes. His canvassing of the neighborhood around the site of a second mass murder at a groceria supplied the vital lead toward identifying the killer.

Afterward, Mackey explained to Vendrell that his son, Matthew, had been diagnosed as being autistic. Vendrell stammered his apologies.

```
Surveillance  Transcript:  085-10365  Location  ref:
FARM-3233
-----------------------------------------------------------
Mackey: It's been tough . . . a lot of work. . . .
The one thing I've learned is . . . I goddamn love
that kid more now than ever. He's got problems . . .
but I'm never giving up on him.

(pause)

I'm not giving up on you either, Shane.
```

Tilt

Some of Vendrell's run-ins with officialdom make for interesting reading. He hits about as often as he misses. There's a wild positive/negative swing to his rhythms.

During a search for Mexican gunrunner Pazi Aranbula, Vendrell went undercover in the clandestine world of illegal cockfighting. Posing as a redneck breeder of fighting birds looking to trade cocks for guns, he lured Pazi to a meeting place.

He and Detective Lemansky fought to subdue Pazi. When chloroform failed, Vendrell clubbed him with a wooden beam. That did the trick.

The original plan had been to wait to bust Pazi until after he'd led them to his store of guns, but Vendrell changed it.

```
Surveillance   Transcript:   073-99102   Location   ref:
FARM-3896
-----------------------------------------------------------------
Lemansky (angrily): Just once, can't we do what we're
supposed to do? You said we were gonna play this one
straight, Shane!

Vendrell: I changed my mind.
```

• • •

About the time when the Quinteros were first making their moves, Long Beach Sheriff's Office deputies pulled over a vehicle at night for speeding. Among the passengers was Mackey's CI, black drug boss Tio. The car also yielded a bag filled with cocaine.

Following Tio's car was a second vehicle, an unmarked car. When the first car was stopped, it pulled over. Two individuals got out, identifying themselves as Vendrell and Lemansky of the Farmington Strike Team.

They said that Tio was their informant and that he was en route to a drug buy, an undercover operation they were running to bust a big dope ring.

The deputies contacted Captain Aceveda at home. He drove down to Long Beach to investigate.

He told the deputies that what Vendrell and Lemansky had said was correct. The deputies dropped the matter, releasing Tio and his crew and the drugs.

Aceveda told Mackey to file the proper paperwork on the operation and went home.

The Wandering Badge Murder put Vendrell back in the doghouse again.

A man holding a police badge used it to get buzzed past the securely locked door of a jewelry store. Once inside, he shot a clerk dead and stole a bag of diamonds, leaving the badge behind.

The badge was no fake. It was authentic. Badge 714, belonging to Detective Shane Vendrell.

Aceveda demanded that Vendrell produce his badge. He couldn't. All he had was an inferior imitation thing. He said that he'd lost his badge and replaced it with a fake.

His badge had finally come home. Aceveda scornfully noted that Vendrell should have known the badge would turn up on the black market, to be used by some crook for a purpose similar to that for which it had been used.

He put Vendrell on suspension for one week and indicated that he was thinking of pulling him off the Strike Team, making room on the squad for that new minority member Lanie Kellis was pushing so hard for.

The murder-robbery turned out to be only the tip of the iceberg. The jewelry store was an "ice chop shop," an Armenian mob operation where stolen jewels were recut into less traceable stones. The killer, Hrach, had been feuding with the clerk, another member of the same mob.

The mob boss was Alex Eznik, head of the Zeroun organized crime family. Catching Hrach, Mackey used him to get to Eznik. Posing as a pair of crooked cops, Mackey and Vendrell got enough on Eznik and his crew to bust them all.

It was an important bust. Mackey used it as a bargaining chip with Aceveda, to keep Vendrell on the team.

Aceveda said okay, but he still intended to put a qualified minority group member on the squad.

Again, Mackey had saved Vendrell's job.

Detective Curtis "Lemonhead" Lemansky

Lemansky was brought onto the team by Shane Vendrell. He's solid, dependable, and more or less even-tempered, unlike the volatile and unpredictable Vendrell (or Mackey for that matter—but Mackey's rages generally seem to have an element of calculation behind them). He's a big, powerful man. When things get physical, Lemansky cracks down hard. He's confident enough not to have to prove anything.

Tigre by the Tail

While bodyguarding beautiful Tigre Orozco, Lemansky became personally involved and showed just how hard he could crack down.

A Los Mags crew led by banger Hector Estanza was hijacking cigarette delivery vans, viciously beating the drivers, and stealing the cargoes. Acting on a tip, Mackey and Lemansky went looking for Estanza associate and LM member Chaco Orozco.

They went to the residence of Estanza's girlfriend and Orozco's sister, Tigre. Chaco Orozco fled out the back door. The officers gave chase. Orozco reached for a weapon. Lemansky opened fire, wounding him. Orozco went to the hospital, while his gun was booked into evidence and stored in the Barn's evidence locker.

Lemansky later learned that Chaco had quit the gang and gone straight and that he'd gone to Tigre's to protect her. She'd broken up with Estanza, who'd burned her to mark her as his property.

With Orozco down, Lemansky guarded seductive, dangerous Tigre. That the assignment was more than a job became evident when Lemansky learned that Estanza had burned Tigre.

Going alone to Estanza's crib, Lemansky gave him a beating. Estanza's crew tried to intervene.

It was fortunate for Lemansky that Mackey and Vendrell happened to be nearby, staking out the place and keeping the bangers under surveillance. They charged in with guns drawn, keeping the bangers at bay.

Later, a police delivery van transporting evidence from the Barn to Central Storage was hijacked by armed robbers, who stole only one item: the gun that Orozco was alleged to have had on his person when apprehended by Mackey and Lemansky.

The van driver noted that the crew boss had the image of a flying snake tattooed on his forearm. The design was one popular with Los Mags members. Indeed, Hector Estanza had one in the same place as the hijacker crew boss.

The Strike Team apprehended Estanza and his crew, finding a gun that had been used in the robbery. Estanza claimed that it was a frame-up and that the gun had been planted. The gun was later identified as the one that had been used to shoot out the van's tires.

The Orozco gun was never recovered. Without it, there was no case against Orozco, and the charges were dropped.

The question remains: since Orozco and Estanza were feuding (there was bad blood between them), why would Estanza go to the trouble of stealing the gun that could send Orozco to jail?

Prosecutors argued that Estanza stole the gun because he wanted to use it as a club to hold over the heads of both Orozcos, brother and sister. By possessing the gun that could send Chaco to jail, Estanza could use it to force Tigre to come back to him. Instead, he and his crew went to prison.

Tigre Orozco had a new boyfriend: Curtis Lemansky.

This investigation has been unable to determine the origin or significance of Lemansky's nickname, "Lemonhead."

Ronald "Ronnie" Gardocki

IAD Surveillance Photo: #131. Subject: Estanza Interrogation.

Like his buddy Lemansky, Ronnie Gardocki was brought into the squad by Shane Vendrell. Gardocki is the technical services guy. He can tap a phone, plant a bug mic, hack into a computer, drive a garbage truck. He handled the wiretapping in the Ara's Pastry drug bust.

Gardocki is no techno-geek. He's tough. Witness the Armadillo case.

Having a price on his head makes a man edgy. Gardocki thought he'd seen a car following him around town a couple of times. He wasn't sure.

He went to Mackey's motel room to drop off some photos. Armadillo and some of his crew caught him there. They were probably lying in wait for Mackey but they took what they could get. They gave him a beating. Then, sending Mackey a message, Armadillo held Gardocki's face down against a hot stovetop electric coil burner, searing his flesh.

Gardocki lived. Eventually his face was somewhat repaired, thanks to extensive skin grafts taken from his left buttock and thigh.

Tavon Garris

Lanie Kellis, the civilian auditor, was not the first person to remark on the unacceptability of having an all-white Strike Team knocking down doors in an 83 percent black and Latino district. Unlike the others, she was in a position to do something about it.

The Strike Team needed a qualified minority group member. As the city council's representative monitoring the Barn, Kellis had the power to make her recommendations stick. In fact, she didn't need to do much of a selling job on Captain Aceveda. He shared her feelings about the negative public image of an elite all-white team cracking down on predominantly black and Latino felons.

Besides, he wanted to have his own set of eyes and ears on the squad. Someone who hadn't been handpicked by Vic Mackey.

Several promising candidates were scared off upon learning that the entire team had been marked for death. It's no accident that Mackey made sure they knew it. He wanted control.

Detective Tavon Garris was made of tougher stuff. The possibility of being marked for death by a murderous drug gang didn't faze him. He wanted in on the team.

He was given a provisional tryout. Lemansky worked with him, liked him, and said admiringly of him, "He's got a mean streak, but it's under control."

Vendrell was not so easily sold. He was doubtful, suspecting that Garris was an undercover agent put in place to spy on the team. Complicating the picture was Vendrell's psychology: he was jealous of anybody else who got close to Mackey.

There have been a racial angle as well: Vendrell's been known to use the N word.

From what he'd seen of Garris, Mackey liked him. He seemed like Mackey's kind of cop. Mackey thought he might work out and wanted to give him a chance. Garris had good connections in the black community. He was handsome, athletic, and a charmer when he wanted to be.

He was also smart, tough, and ruthless.

On April 1 of this year, the Johnnies street gang was on a mission to kill three innocent civilians at random, one for each gang member killed in the previous year. The first victim was Jeff Franklin, Detective Claudette Wyms's ex-husband.

Mackey and Garris located Johnnies gang leader Lops. Lops didn't want to talk. Garris emptied all the slugs but one from his revolver, pointed it at Lops's head, spun the chamber, and pulled the trigger.

The hammer clicked on an empty. One or two more spins of the chamber and Lops was ready to talk.

Handcuffed, being taken away, Lops was unable to resist the urge to boast. He told Garris that the cops were too late, that a Johnnies shooter was en route to a local street fair, to randomly slay a citizen.

It wasn't too late. Garris tipped Mackey, and the two of them, plus uniformed backup units, were able to apprehend the would-be killer before he struck.

Lanie Kellis approached Garris, trying to persuade him to be her informant on the team.

He refused the offer.

4. CAPTAIN
DAVID ACEVEDA

```
Surveillance   Transcript:   077-12185   Location   ref:
FARM-6571
------------------------------------------------------------
Aceveda: In this building, I'm in charge.
```

New Breed

When Ben Gilroy was putting together the Farmington station, he got everything he wanted—except the power to name the new division captain. His candidates were all rejected by his boss, the then-chief of police, who reserved the right to appoint the captain. He wanted his own man in there, not Gilroy's.

Perhaps even then he suspected that it would be a good idea to have someone looking over Gilroy's shoulder. He chose David Segovia Aceveda for the captain's post.

Aceveda was one of the new breed of cops, less of a traditional street cop and more of a well-educated managerial type. (He was derided as a "test-taker" by Vic Mackey.)

As it turned out, Aceveda proved to be neither Gilroy's man nor the chief's man. He was his own man. A man with big ideas. A man with a plan. His idea was to use the department as a springboard toward a political career. For him, the department is not an end but a means. That makes him dangerous.

It means that, in a crisis, he might put his own ambitions ahead of the department. Indeed, the way he ultimately resolved the 911 riots, the Gilroy affair, and the Kellis report to his own benefit shows that he's looking out for number one.

Unfortunately, at this late date, it will be difficult to get him under control. Especially now that he's got his own constituency, his own media contacts. He's media savvy and knows how to play to the press.

Assuming the post of captain of the Barn was a calculated risk on Aceveda's part. If the precinct was a success (success being defined as a

National Organization
of United Police Officers

The National Organization of United Police Officers is proud to award this document to an officer who has met all of the standards set forth by our fine organization.

Our organization was founded on the platform that there exists a common thread that unites all police officers under one cloak of thought : the protection of the general public at large.

Regardless of the location, race, or color, the connecting thread binds police officer to police officer into a brotherhood with a common thought, goal, and purpose, that of protecting the public.

Therefore, as police officers, let us all embrace one another and form a family united in the idea that our function relative to the public is to protect, honor, and serve.

Awarded to

David Aceveda

discernible drop in district crime stats), he would be in a position to reap the positive publicity. If the experiment failed, he'd have to take the rap for it, essentially ending his career in the department. Aceveda's sights, however, were trained on other goals.

IAD Surveillance Photo: #131. Subject: Crowley/Aceveda connection.

Death of a Detective

Although Aceveda was Mackey's boss, Mackey liked to think of himself as having carved out his own independent piece of turf. His career-long history of tangling with authority figures ensured that he'd be butting heads with Aceveda. He relied on his connections with Gilroy to offset the captain's influence.

After its first four months up and running, the precinct was a definite success. A mainstay of that success was the Strike Team, with its stellar arrest and conviction rate. With it came a large number of complaints about excessive force, coercion, brutality, and even corruption.

Aceveda wanted an in on the squad. It was provided courtesy of Detective Terry Crowley.

Aceveda and Crowley were more than brother cops—they were longtime friends. It was Aceveda who'd convinced Crowley to leave his post in Robbery Division to transfer into the Strike Team. Crowley didn't need much persuading. It was a plum assignment, better than the one he currently occupied.

He made the jump.

For the few months he served on the team, he was an outsider, the only one who didn't have a personal connection to somebody else on the squad. The fact that Aceveda had put him in did not inspire confidence in the others, who worried that he might be reporting on them back to the captain.

So they kept him on the outside, assigning him such tasks as driving and doing routine legwork, but none of the gritty, down-and-dangerous assignments like going undercover or taking part in raids.

After the precinct had been in operation for about four months, Crowley was ready to make his move. He suggested to Mackey that he could do a lot more, be a useful asset, if Mackey would let him on the inside.

Mackey received a tip that drug dealer Two-Time was holding a cache of drugs at his residence. A warrant was obtained, and the Strike Team set out on a nighttime raid. Crowley was on board. This was the first time he'd be going into real action with the team.

The team went in without backup. Mackey later explained that this was done to keep the operation close and tight, to keep from alerting Two-Time of their approach.

Two-Time lived in a single-family house. The ground-floor windows were barred; the door was reinforced. The Strike Team used a ladder to enter via a second-floor window at the rear of the house.

Two-Time was not alone. With him was a girlfriend. Hearing the sounds of the break-in, he took a bag of drugs and a handgun with him to the bathroom. He was trying to dump the drugs down the toilet when the Strike Team came upon him. Identifying themselves as police, they or-dered him to freeze.

What happened next is a matter of some dispute.

According to the official Strike Team report, Two-Time opened fire, down-ing Crowley. Mackey and Vendrell returned fire, killing Two-Time.

As per standard operating procedure, Crowley, like the other team mem-bers, was wearing a protective Kevlar vest. Unfortunately, he'd been shot in the face. One of Two-Time's bullets had hit him in the cheek, below the left eye.

After being shot, he never spoke a word. It's doubtful whether he was con-scious, and if so, if he was even aware of his surroundings. He was taken to the hospital, where he died a few hours later.

Two-Time was already DOA—Dead on Arrival.

An IAD investigation found that Crowley's death had occurred as a conse-quence of his duties. No censure or reprimand was given to any of the Strike Team members or their supervisory personnel.

However, there were some facts that never reached the IAD sleuths.

Facts collected by this investigation.

• • •

An SIU confidential source in the Los Angeles branch of the U.S. Department of Justice (DOJ) has provided certain information relating to the death of Detective Terry Crowley.

Shortly before the raid, DOJ agent Moses Hernandez spoke with his supervisor about the possibility of arranging a DOJ job for Detective Crowley. The arrangement was predicated on Crowley's ability to help break a case involving alleged high-level police corruption in the Farmington Division.

Specifically, he was targeted against Vic Mackey and the Strike Team, who were suspected of major involvement in district drug trafficking. The team was accused of taking money to protect favored drug dealers from arrest while harrassing and arresting their dope business competitors.

Hernandez said that Crowley told him he'd seen Mackey and Vendrell "conferring" with drug gang leader Rondell Robinson. Crowley had agreed to try to get the goods on Mackey and company, but in return, he wanted a future with the DOJ. He knew that exposing even a dirty cop would finish him in the department.

He'd be in career Siberia.

According to our source, such an arrangement could be brokered only through DOJ higher-ups at headquarters in Washington, D.C. Agent Hernandez had to go through channels. He put in the request and the deal was in the process of being made.

Before it could be finalized, Crowley was dead, killed during the raid.

Also dead was the DOJ probe into the Strike Team. The investigation had been only tentative at best, a case of the L.A. branch of the DOJ putting out feelers as a prelude to launching a federal anticorruption probe of the city police.

A probe that would do the department no good.

It should be noted here that Hernandez and Aceveda are old friends, going back to their college days together at USC. It was Aceveda who'd put Crowley together with Hernandez.

In this, Aceveda was acting on his own. Departmental protocol required that he notify IAD that he was initiating such an investigation. The record shows that no such notification was made. Aceveda put himself way out on a limb.

He was in violation of departmental procedures, which could render him liable to disciplinary actions. However, especially at this late date, there's no way to bring Aceveda up on departmental charges without reopening a case that's better left closed.

• • •

Further light was shone on this murky business by Ben Gilroy. While under house arrest, awaiting trial on hit-and-run and fraud charges, Gilroy met several times with Lanie Kellis.

Gilroy told her that he'd had a friend in the local DOJ branch who'd told him that Detective Crowley planned to work undercover against the Strike Team. This was the first the DOJ official had heard about it, and he wanted to know why his buddy Gilroy hadn't given him a heads-up about it.

It was the first Gilroy had heard about it, too. He pretended otherwise, smoothing things out. As soon as he could, he contacted Mackey, tipping him off that Crowley was an undercover informant.

Shortly after that, Crowley went out on his first raid with the Strike Team and was killed.

What really happened on the raid?

On several occasions in public, Aceveda has been overheard making strong allusions to his belief that Vic Mackey was somehow directly involved in Crowley's death. Once, for over an hour and a half, behind the closed doors of the interrogation room, he and Detective Dutch Wagenbach grilled Shane Vendrell about the raid. Vendrell maintained that it had all gone down just the way he and the others had told it. Mackey arrived, ending the session.

Tensions ran so hot between Aceveda and Mackey that Gilroy came down to the Barn to intervene. He warned Aceveda that if he continued his "pissing contest" with "my best detective [Mackey]," Gilroy would have to decide between the two men, and Aceveda wouldn't like his choice.

Power of the Press

Aceveda wasn't intimidated. His next opportunity to go after Mackey came not by design but by chance, when Officer Julien Lowe walked into his office and reported that he'd seen Mackey and Vendrell steal two bricks of cocaine during the Ara's Pastry drug bust. Lowe wrote out a statement, which was given to IAD, triggering an investigation into the charges.

Learning that Vendrell had gone out on a wild, gun-toting rampage seeking his stolen Navigator SUV, Aceveda guessed there was more to it than a matter of a stolen vehicle. When apprehended, the car thief said that she'd found two bricks of cocaine in the SUV and passed them on to her boyfriend.

Aceveda got to him too late. He was dead of a cocaine overdose, but no drugs were found on the premises.

Point to Mackey.

A further setback stung Aceveda when Julien Lowe retracted his statement about seeing Mackey and Vendrell steal the drugs. Aceveda, furious, was sure that Mackey had somehow gotten to Lowe to get him to withdraw the charges.

Proof? He had none.

Lowe's retraction killed the IAD probe.

ngeles Times

PRECINCT ROCKED

Los Angeles–Farmington Precinct was rocked today with the announcement that two officers in their special unit squad internally known as the Strike Team, were being investigated for the alleged theft of narcotics seized at a crime scene Detectives Vic Mackey and Shane Vendrell were named by Internal Affairs Division (IAD) as being complicit in the

Someone leaked details of the IAD's confidential investigation to the press. It was front-page news, naming the members of the Strike Team as suspected drug thieves. A black eye for them, the precinct, and the department.

Gilroy hastened to the Barn, where he confronted Aceveda. "Chief dunked my balls like a couple of doughnuts in his morning coffee," Gilroy said, alluding to the chief of police's reaction to seeing the headlines in the day's papers.

Gilroy accused Aceveda of being the leak. Aceveda's denials were apparently less than convincing, at least to Gilroy. Gilroy told him that no one in the department had gotten anywhere careerwise by being "anticop."

He said that Aceveda was finished in the department, washed up. Aceveda countered by saying that as far as the public was concerned, firing him would only validate the corruption charges.

Gilroy said that Aceveda "had thought it all out," but warned him not to overreach himself.

He left.

The follow-up showed that Aceveda had been playing a deep game.

Earlier, he'd struck up an acquaintance with Latino political powerhouse Jorge Machado, asking for his support to make a run for the Sixth District's city council seat. Machado was initially cool to the idea. Aceveda was a Latino, and Latino voters held a plurality in the district. He was potentially an attractive candidate: educated, telegenic, media savvy, a young, fresh face. His wife, Aurora, and their baby girl were also assets for anyone aspiring to public office.

However, Farmington voters were generally none too fond of the police.

Still, Machado said he'd think it over.

Then news of the alleged Strike Team drug theft hit the papers. The coverage painted Aceveda as a hero, a reformer who was trying to get dirty cops off the street. (In fact, the favorable press was what had convinced Gilroy that Aceveda was the leaker.)

As it turned out, Aceveda was the leaker, but only indirectly. He'd passed a copy of the IAD file to Latino community activist Raoul Jimenez, who knew where to place it to do the most good. Jimenez arranged for the story to get a big play in the papers.

This gave a boost to Aceveda's chances in the city council race, allowing Machado's spin doctors and image makers to portray Aceveda as a heroic, anticorruption cop who fights crime wherever he finds it, even when it's hiding behind a badge.

The publicity tipped the scales. Machado decided to support Aceveda's bid for city council. An announcement date and kickoff day was set for May 5, Cinco de Mayo.

When Officer Julien Lowe changed his statement, IAD dropped its investigation into Mackey's coke theft. However, Machado believed that what remained in the public's mind were the original positive headlines, not their refutation later.

He was still strongly committed to backing Aceveda.

Cry Rape

Candidate Aceveda soon learned that a man running for office is a target. However, moving targets are harder to hit.

His political career threatened to stall and crash almost immediately after takeoff, due to the threat posed by Tereza Varela, a reporter for the Spanish-language newspaper *La Unidad*.

Digging into Aceveda's background, Varela came in contact with Maureen Wilmore. Daughter of powerful publisher Chester Wilmore, she alleged that fifteen years ago, when they were both students at USC, she'd been raped by Aceveda.

He'd tied her up, choked her, and raped her, she said. Even after the rape, he'd continued to stalk her, until his harassment became so menacing that she was forced to defend herself with a knife, slashing him with it to fend him off.

Confronted at the Barn by Varela, Aceveda denied the charges and warned her not to print them.

While refusing to comment publicly on the story, Aceveda spoke of it in private. According to a source close to Machado, Aceveda said that the truth was that it was Maureen Wilmore who'd been stalking him at USC.

They'd been casual (he thought) lovers, but when he'd tried to break up with her, she'd become obsessed with him, following and harassing him, ultimately attacking him with a penknife belonging to his college dorm roommate.

Shortly before her article could appear, Tereza Varela was fired from *La Unidad*. Informed sources say that Aceveda's power broker and patron, Jorge Machado, was instrumental in having her lose her job. Machado is a longtime associate and friend of the publisher of *La Unidad*.

Undaunted, Varela went freelance, submitting the article to the *Times*. It is known that, around this time, Aceveda visited Maureen Wilmore at her residence on two separate occasions.

After the first, she continued to stick to her story of the rape. After the second, she made a 180-degree turn, repudiating the story and refusing further comment. Without her statement, there was no story, as the *Times* editors informed Varela when they told her they were dropping it.

How and why Aceveda got Wilmore to back off from her story may only be guessed.

It may be worth noting that, to this day, he still bears the scar from the knife wound inflicted on him by Maureen Wilmore.

```
Surveillance  Transcript:  335-58007  Location  ref:
FARM-2535
---------------------------------------------------------------
Mackey (to Aceveda): Keep smiling for the cameras.
See what you can do about getting the men's john
fixed.
```

In fact, Aceveda got the women's john fixed. As the only working toilet facility in the Barn, it was used by both sexes. Then the pipes burst, flooding the first floor, leaving the Barn with no working toilets.

Aceveda called in a twenty-four-hour-on-duty plumber to fix the mess. The bill came to $800. He charged it on his credit card.

He's still waiting to be reimbursed by the department.

He's liable to be waiting for a long, long time.

Gilroy Was Here

Two Days of Blood threatened to sink not only Aceveda's candidacy but also the precinct itself.

Two Days of Blood is shorthand for the series of events that began with the murder of two women an hour after they'd called 911 for help, ripening into forty-eight hours of rioting and the ambush murders of three police officers.

After the first ambush killings, Gilroy and his headquarters entourage set up shop in the Barn, taking over Aceveda's office and relegating him to the sidelines. It was all part of his plan to make Aceveda the fall guy for the disasters.

As we now know, Gilroy had bigger fish to fry than hanging the mess on Aceveda. He was covering up his involvement in a fatal hit-and-run and in diverting division resources to leave the Grove underpoliced, creating a crime wave he could exploit as part of a massive real estate scheme.

In any case, Aceveda wasn't sitting still.

When Detective Claudette Wyms got a lead on the location of the 911 woman killer Wally Forton, Aceveda made sure to be present at the arrest.

Meanwhile, Mackey and Wagenbach were both working the hit-and-run case. When they began closing in on Sedona Tellez, the passenger in the car, Gilroy decided it was time to burn his old buddy Vic.

Gilroy went to Aceveda, saying that perhaps Aceveda had been right all along in distrusting Mackey, that Mackey was a crooked cop. He wanted Aceveda to apply for a search warrant for Mackey's home residence. He didn't know that Aceveda was playing a double game.

Aceveda had already been approached—by Mackey.

Mackey put forward the proposition that both he and Aceveda had an enemy in common: Gilroy. Moreover, he said he had something on Gilroy. Sedona Tellez, the passenger in the blue Mercedes, was Gilroy's girlfriend. Together, they'd conspired to work up a massive real estate fraud scheme.

The intricate financial manipulations were out of Mackey's league, he said. But Aceveda had the "smarts" to follow the paper and money trail and smoke out the details of the scheme.

For the moment, he and Aceveda were on the same side.

Like the Hitler-Stalin pact.

When the Strike Team located the last two 911 ambush killers, Aceveda went in with them to make the arrests. Mackey didn't see the female shooter, Twanya, taking a bead on him with a gun. Aceveda did, and shot her dead—saving Mackey's life.

Benji, the other shooter, was taken alive.

Aceveda was able to crack Gilroy's real estate scam. He discovered that Sedona Tellez had illegally parked police department funds in offshore accounts to buy properties. Sedona flipped, giving up Gilroy.

Gilroy was arrested and charged with fraud and manslaughter.

Aceveda came out of the dung heap covered with diamonds.

New Highs

Post-riot, Aceveda's capture of the 911 ambush killers and arrest of Gilroy gave him a fifteen- to seventeen-point lead in the polls over rival candidate Karen Mitchell. He'd made enemies on the city council—they didn't like him making a silk purse out of a sow's ear. They sent Civilian Auditor Lanie Kellis to monitor doings at the Barn.

But her real mission, Aceveda felt, was to get something on him that would sink his candidacy.

In the Gilroy affair and afterward, Aceveda was forced to make a Faustian bargain with Mackey. To clinch the primary election, he needed to keep crime stats down and keep a lid on any potential Barn scandals. With Kellis on the scene, sniffing around for any scent of wrongdoing, he had to do what he could to make sure that the Strike Team's dirty laundry stayed carefully hidden.

Not trust but mutual self-interest cemented the alliance with Mackey. But it would be subjected to intense pressure from all sides.

```
Surveillance   Transcript:   023-92584  Location  ref:
FARM-7458
--------------------------------------------------------------
Aceveda (to Mackey): By this time next year, I'm
going to be on the city council. In six years, I'm
going to be mayor. By then, I'll have much bigger
problems than you.
```

Cop for a Day

Departmental policy mandates that all precinct plainclothes administrative personnel must periodically work a shift in uniform on street patrol. Not even captains are exempt from this ruling.

On one such recent tour of duty, David Aceveda donned his police blues and went on patrol with Officer Julien Lowe. They responded to a complaint from a woman who said that her son's new bike had been stolen. Driving through the neighborhood, they noticed a youngster riding a bicycle matching the description of the stolen bike. The boy said that it was his bike.

Aceveda confiscated the bike, giving the youth a strict talking-to and warning him not to steal again. He and Lowe returned the bike to the original complainants, only to learn that it was the wrong one—it lacked the identifying marks borne by the genuine article.

Aceveda and Lowe went looking for the boy from whom they'd confiscated the bike. Aceveda sheepishly returned the bike to him, with many apologies. Covering for him, Julien explained that Aceveda was a rookie and asked that allowances be made for his lack of experience.

The boy who was the victim of the theft did not go away empty-handed. He got a bike, too—Aceveda bought him a duplicate of the one he'd lost.

Heroin School Daze

Aceveda's comfortable fifteen-point lead was threatened by a heroin epidemic targeting schoolchildren. Behind it lay Armadillo's drug mob, looking for new markets to exploit.

Quick to try to capitalize on the situation was Karen Mitchell, Aceveda's rival for the party's city council primary slot. An assistant to powerful Councilman Morgan, she'd also been quick to jump in during the community unrest in the Grove over the 911 killings.

Now, at the height of the heroin epidemic, she held a press conference on the steps of one of the affected schools, using the occasion to denounce the Barn in general and Aceveda in particular for failing to stop dope pushers from moving in on the children.

When the Strike Team stood ready to make the swoop and come down on Armadillo, he arranged to surrender to Aceveda instead. As it turned out, Armadillo didn't live long. He was soon stabbed to death by another prisoner in the Barn holding cell.

It was messy, sloppy, and generated bad press. Still, it soon all blew over. Nobody was mourning the loss of Armadillo, a child rapist and sadistic killer who'd even unblinkingly ordered the murder of his own brother.

What Aceveda knew of the extent and details of the relationship between Armadillo and Mackey can only be guessed at. Still, he can hardly have been too upset by Armadillo's passing.

Dead men tell no tales.

Deep Cuts

As primary election day neared, the preliminary Kellis report was leaked to the press, precipitating a minicrisis at headquarters.

Word came down from the top: Aceveda would stay in command of the Barn until primary day. Chief Bankston met with Aceveda to lay out the options.

If Aceveda won, he'd be moving up and out.

If he lost, he would submit his resignation, saying he needed to spend more time with his family. That's what they always say in situations like this.

Aceveda agreed. What else could he do?

Soon enough headquarters brass would find out just what else exactly he could do, and they wouldn't like it.

On top of everything else, with a new round of budget cuts looming, the precinct workforce had to be cut by 20 percent.

The dirty job of deciding who would stay and who must go was tossed into Aceveda's lap. He'd have to make the cuts, and tell officers who needed the job (and they all needed the job) that they didn't have one.

With the primary race shaping up as a close call, Aceveda's campaign manager, Jorge Machado, urged him to attend some last-minute rallies on the night before election day. The few hundred votes thus gained could spell the difference between victory and defeat. Aceveda refused, electing to stay at his post.

He still had one last trick up his sleeve. He had no bridges to burn with the department; he'd already burned them all.

Instead of making the required cuts, he sent a letter to Chief Bankston's office.

It contained a list of the names of five persons responsible for the chaos and disorder in the precinct, a list of five who should be fired.

The list read:

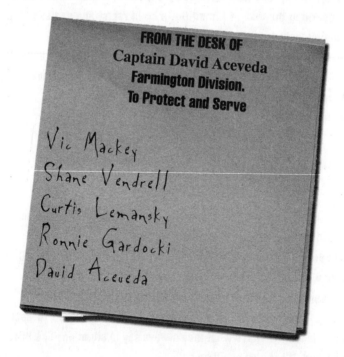

Aceveda went into primary day four points down in the polls. He voted early. A TV news crew caught him at the polling place. An interviewer asked him about the list, which had already created a buzz at police headquarters and City Hall.

Aceveda had also given copies of the list to the *Times* and other media outlets, to ensure that the department couldn't bury it. This was the one way to make sure the department would have to confront the problems with the Strike Team.

Why, the reporter inquired, had Aceveda included his own name on the list?

Because he was the precinct head, and had to take the responsibility for what had gone wrong in the division, Aceveda said.

His reply was made early enough in the day to be run several times on various local news programs while the voting was still in progress. Maybe that's what made the difference, because at the finish, after the polls had closed, David Aceveda was declared the winner of the Sixth Council District primary.

Next stop: election day in November.

5. DETECTIVE CLAUDETTE WYMS

```
Surveillance  Transcript:  138-95817  Location  ref:
FARM-6151
--------------------------------------------------------
Claudette Wyms (to Dutch Wagenbach): I don't need a
"special team." I'll do my own police work.
```

Claudette Wyms is a good cop and a smart detective. Too smart not to notice when something dirty is going on right under her nose. That put her at odds with Vic Mackey—and Captain Aceveda.

But not at first. For months she looked away, ignoring the evidence of Strike Team brutality and the rumors of corruption and even worse. Until finally she couldn't look away anymore and made it her business to find the truth and do whatever had to be done.

• • •

Farmington File Photo: Det. Wyms assists arrest Case #36-940-A3.

Claudette Wyms followed a roundabout path to a career in California law enforcement. Her father, a college professor of English literature, Professor Bryce Wyms, who is still living, described his daughter as "a brilliant scholar." As a teenager, she had studied classical dance for nine months in Paris. He was surprised and perhaps a bit disappointed when she decided on a career in law enforcement.

(Now he's more proud of her than ever.)

Claudette got into police work because that was where she could make a difference. She came up through the ranks, from patrol officer to detective. A black woman in a macho police culture. She was tough enough not to have to raise her voice to get things done.

Whether you are male or female, police work is rough on marriages. Wyms has been married twice and divorced twice. She has two grown daughters: Rebecca, a Boston schoolteacher, and Bonnie, a Florida reporter. She owns a big dog.

She's currently single.

Dutch Treat?

When the Barn was formed, Wyms was one of the first detectives selected to serve in the district. On day one, before any of the detectives were yet partnered up, she met Detective Holland "Dutch" Wagenbach.

Their first meeting was hardly auspicious.

Wagenbach was starstruck in the presence of senior detective Tom Gannon, a legend in the department for having cracked the Beechwood Canyon Slasher case. Wyms hardly registered on his radar.

Sometimes lacking in social skills, Wagenbach tactlessly said, on being introduced to Wyms, "I've never heard of you."

She'd never heard of him, either, but was too polite to say so.

Before too long, Wagenbach would be saying admiringly, "Wow—how come I never heard of you?"

```
Surveillance  Transcript:  013-20225  Location  ref:
FARM-0018
------------------------------------------------------------
Claudette Wyms (to Dutch): Credit's overrated.
```

Wyms didn't have a flashy rep. That was because she was results-oriented, more interested in solving the case than in who gets the credit. But insiders know that she's one of the top detectives on the force.

That first day, she and Wagenbach worked the case of a vicious crew of kidnappers who preyed on Salvadoran immigrants. Wyms felt certain that the key to the case was Latigo, a ransom broker, a lawyer who specialized in handling the negotiations between kidnappers and victims' families. She convinced him to cooperate. He delivered the ransom. When the gang picked it up, they were busted.

Impressed, Wagenbach suggested that they partner up.

Wyms agreed, Aceveda okayed it, and the partnership had begun.

Wyms on Strike

Months passed. Wyms didn't have much call to interface with the Strike Team. She knew Mackey and his crew played rough, rougher than she cared to. She tried to steer clear of them and their work as much as possible.

Like sausage-making, how the Strike Team made their high arrest rate was a matter best not inquired into too closely. Anyone who undertook the task would need a strong stomach. But when Aceveda locked horns with Mackey, Wyms took it on herself to offer the captain some unsolicited advice.

```
Surveillance  Transcript:  085-31039  Location  ref:
FARM-6652
----------------------------------------------------------------
Wyms: Right now Vic Mackey must look like a mighty
big catch to you. Do the smart thing, though, son.
Cut bait.

Aceveda: It doesn't bother you, the things he does?

Wyms: I don't judge other cops.

Aceveda: Mackey's not a cop. He's Al Capone with a
badge.

Wyms: Al Capone made money by giving people what they
wanted. What people want these days is to make it to
their cars without getting mugged. Come home from
work, see their stereo still there. Hear about some
murder in the barrio, find out the next day the police
caught the guy. If having all those things means some
cop roughs up some nigger or some spick in the
ghetto . . . well, as far as most people are con-
cerned, it's don't ask, don't tell.
```

During the IAD probe into alleged drug thefts, Strike Team activities were temporarily suspended, with team members being paired with other precinct detectives. Wyms found herself being partnered up with Mackey in the investigation of a methamphetamine ring that was dealing drugs at the local college.

This brand of crank was sold in packets marked with an image of Cupid from a child's rubber-stamp kit. A potent, high-velocity mix, it had been cooked up by an out-of-work software programmer and some of his buddies.

He'd managed to cook himself up, too.

Cooking crank is a dangerous business. The chemical ingredients have a tendency to explode. This batch did, horribly burning the amateur chemist, causing him to die a slow, agonizing death.

It was also potent to a toxic degree, sending college kids screaming into the emergency rooms and psycho wards.

Behind the amateur drugmakers who'd cooked up the mess lay Manny Sandoval, a midlevel loan shark and gangster. Wyms and Mackey caught Sandoval but were unable to find the drug cache. That gave Sandoval a bargaining chip. He was able to deal for immunity, to walk away with no charges filed, in exchange for tipping the detectives to the location of the drugs.

With Sandoval penned in a Barn holding cell, Mackey was unable to use his usual strong-arm tactics to persuade Sandoval to talk.

But the crank was too dangerous to be allowed to circulate, to derange more speed freaks.

Sandoval walked—but the drugs were taken off the street.

More Burning Men

A rubber tire doused with gasoline is placed around a bound victim's neck and set on fire, inflicting a hideous burning death. That's the murder mode known as necklacing.

When a number of charred necklaced corpses began turning up in the Farm, it was a sign that Armadillo Quintero was in town.

Quintero's goal was to unite the district's Latino gangs under his leadership and monopolize the area drug trade. Higher-ups in such gangs as the Toros and Los Mags were "invited" to join Armadillo's operation. Those who refused were made examples of, necklaced and burned to death as a warning to others.

One such victim was banger Cuca Reyes.

Detectives Wyms and Wagenbach were on the case. They learned that before he was murdered, Cuca's Anglo girlfriend had been kidnapped and raped by Armadillo. To mark the occasion, he had an image of a dove tattooed on her cheek.

Cuca still refused to go along with Armadillo. Soon after, he was murdered—burned to death. The detectives interviewed Cuca's family, his mother, brother, and twelve-year-old sister, Mayda. Mother and brother refused to talk.

Later, though, Mayda came to the Barn and told Dutch Wagenbach that Armadillo had first made a show of befriending Cuca and the rest of the family. That was during the courting process, early on when he was trying to convince Cuca to join him. Later, Mayda had heard him threaten to kill Cuca if he didn't get with the program.

When Claudette Wyms learned that Dutch had gotten the girl to talk, she didn't like it. Being a witness in a gang murder is no place for a young girl to be. She made Wagenbach break off talks and took the girl home.

Later, Armadillo was picked up and brought in for questioning. He was put in a Barn interrogation room and questioned by Wagenbach. He wouldn't talk, except to deny any involvement in criminal activities.

There were no real charges on which to hold him, and after a few hours his lawyer showed up at the station and secured his release.

Checking up on Mayda, Wyms learned that the girl was missing. When the girl finally arrived at

Farmington File Photo: Armadillo Quintero interrogation 4-1.

home, she was numb, traumatized—and bore a freshly tattooed dove on her cheek.

Mayda's family swiftly spirited her out of the country and into Mexico.

With no victim, there was no case against Armadillo.

Part of Armadillo's plan included muscling out rival drug dealers. His thugs burned down a building owned by one Theodore Osmond, a/k/a. Tio. The same Tio who was one of Vic Mackey's informants. And maybe more than that.

The charred wreckage contained drug scales, cocaine traces, and a fireproof safe. The case fell to Claudette Wyms, but Mackey was working it, too. Aceveda initially showed a preference to have Mackey work the case alone. With an upcoming election, candidate Aceveda couldn't risk having another Mackey scandal surface.

But he didn't want to be seen ordering Claudette Wyms off the case. Especially not with Civilian Auditor Lanie Kellis watching like a hawk for any hint of irregularities. Instead, he ordered Mackey and Wyms to work the case together, setting in motion a mechanism that would eventually put them at each other's throats.

Claudette Wyms wouldn't be able to look the other way when it came to the Strike Team for much longer.

During the arson investigation, Mackey acted like he had something to hide. And Claudette had a pretty good idea of what that was. From

Theodore "Tio" Osmond, Mackey's informant—and maybe more.

the start, Mackey made a number of false steps that showed that something wasn't kosher.

When he and Wyms went to Tio's house to bring him in for questioning, Mackey insisted on going in alone. That was contrary to standard procedure, which in such situations mandates the presence of another officer for backup.

Mackey gave Wyms some lame explanation along the lines that since Tio was his CI, he needed to approach him first, so as not to lose the informant's trust and confidence. Wyms waited outside, steaming, while Mackey went into the house.

He was in there talking to Tio for some time. What they said was unknown to Wyms.

The next false step involved a fireproof safe and a locksmith named Smith, a departmental expert in lock picking and safecracking. Mackey brought in Smith to open the safe.

Tools in hand, Smith began to start to crack into the safe from the front. Wyms had been studying up on that particular model safe and had learned that it was an executive corporate-security safe, which, if tampered with from the front, would break a vial of acid that would destroy the safe's contents.

She called Smith on it. Flustered, he said that he'd made a mistake. He cracked open the safe the correct way, from the rear.

It yielded a ledger, with coded entries showing sums of money incoming and outgoing.

One frequent entry showed payments being made to someone identified as "Landlord." But Tio had no landlord to pay; he owned the building. Wyms guessed that the payments were instead made by Tio to his boss on the next level of the drug-dealing pyramid.

The identity of that higher-up was as yet unknown.

While Wyms was absent from the station, Aceveda ordered Tio released. He was allowed to take his ledger with him. Learning what had been done, Claudette was hopping mad.

Were Aceveda and Mackey in collusion? It certainly looked that way. Wyms let them both know that she didn't like what had gone down and that she was going to find the truth, no matter what.

Soon after, Tio was found necklaced and burned to death. Before his murder, he hadn't had time to destroy the ledger, which was found among his property.

For a second time, the ledger came into Claudette's hands.

Going to Aceveda, she requested an authorization allowing her to examine Mackey's financial records, with an eye toward comparing the dates of his bank deposits with corresponding dates in the ledger recording Tio's payments to "Landlord."

Aceveda okayed the request.

Wyms was unable to find any correlation between the payments and Mackey's funds.

Kingpins

A Mackey initiative enabled Wyms to bag a criminal who'd already escaped her once on a technicality.

That was Manny Sandoval, the loan shark who'd traded his knowledge of where a load of deadly Cupid meth was stashed in exchange for going free on any related charges.

Thanks to Mackey's Toys for Guns ploy, one of the guns turned in was linked to the murder of Richard Cummings, who'd been delinquent in paying back $50,000 he owed to Sandoval. The gun tracked back to a man named Lance Hinkle, who also owed an undisclosed amount to Sandoval. Hinkle's daughter had brought in the gun. She didn't like guns. Toys were better.

When Hinkle was put in a holding cell with Sandoval, the latter warned him to keep his mouth shut, and thereby incriminated himself in the kill.

It was a trap—Wyms had rigged Hinkle with a wire, recording Sandoval's incriminating statements.

Sandoval wouldn't be walking free this time.

After Armadillo put hits out on the Strike Team, someone tried to break into the Mackey house. Corrine, frightened, brought the kids to the Barn. Vic Mackey was out of the station at the time.

While waiting for her husband to arrive, Corrine was taken aside by Claudette Wyms for a private talk that turned into a subtle interrogation. Wyms learned that Corrine was unaware of her husband's doings, that she knew nothing of Armadillo or the hits. Wyms fished around for financial irregularities. About all she could come up with was Matthew's $25,000-a-year tuition at Glen Ridge special-needs school.

Corrine said she thought Vic put in lots of overtime to meet expenses.

"That's what he tells you," Wyms said skeptically.

Mackey arrived, barging in and ending the interview. He raged that, by questioning his wife, Wyms had crossed a line she shouldn't have crossed. Undeterred, Claudette Wyms refused to apologize—or to back off.

The growing hostility between her and Mackey had at last erupted into the open.

```
Surveillance  Transcript:  075-03572  Location  ref:
FARM-2001
-----------------------------------------------------------------
Corrine (to Vic): I got more truth from her in ten
minutes than I've gotten from you in a year!
```

The beating and burning torture of Strike Team member Ronnie Gardocki brought the war with Armadillo to fever pitch. Wyms couldn't help noticing that Armadillo seemed to have "a thing for burning." She recalled that a search of Armadillo's abandoned house had revealed traces of human flesh adhering to a stovetop burner.

Her offer of help in tracking down Armadillo was summarily rejected by Mackey. "Don't take this the wrong way, but I can handle this by myself," he said.

When Armadillo surrendered, Wyms—who hadn't seen him since the time several months earlier when she'd been investigating Cuca's murder—now saw that Quintero bore burn marks on his cheek virtually identical to those that had been inflicted on Ronnie Gardocki.

Had Gardocki's burning been payback in kind for what had been done to Armadillo? Had Armadillo been burned by a member of the Strike Team?

She knew Mackey wasn't above beating and torturing a suspect to get what he wanted. He'd beaten Dr. Grady into revealing where he'd hidden abducted eight-year-old Jenny Reborg. He'd allegedly tortured 911 shooter Sonny with the pin of a slain officer's badge to find the identities of the other two shooters.

Then Armadillo was stabbed to death by another prisoner in the holding cell.

How had the killer, Pinto, gotten the knife?

Earlier, he'd been arrested for smoking reefers by Officer Danielle "Danny" Sofer. Sofer had searched him before locking him in the cell, and insisted that she couldn't have overlooked an item as large as a knife. She thought that Pinto might have been passed the knife by another prisoner.

Wyms asked her if the knife couldn't have been passed by a cop.

What cop would have benefitted from Armadillo's death?

A Strike Team cop.

Danny Sofer wasn't ready to consider the possibility. Wyms shrugged. Sofer had asked her for help in fighting the charge that it was her negligence that had led to Armadillo's death.

Wyms had done her best to wise Danny up. If Danny Sofer didn't want to face facts, that was her business.

Claudette Wyms went back to work.

She had a job to do.

New Broom?

Prior to release of her report on precinct abuses, Lanie Kellis privately approached Claudette Wyms. She said that her report would put the Strike Team and what she perceived as an alliance between Mackey and Aceveda at the center of the division's problems. But it would praise Wyms's performance.

Kellis would recommend to her council patrons that Wyms be made captain of the precinct.

Claudette said flatly that she didn't want the job.

She changed her mind after the Jeffrey Cole case. Fourteen-year-old Jeffrey Cole had been reported missing. It was feared that he'd fallen victim to a serial killer who liked to abduct, rape, and murder pairs of teen boys in tandem.

A prime suspect was Adam, a convicted pedophile then currently at large.

Mackey thought that the boy might be hidden in Adam's house. To enter, he needed probable cause that a crime was being committed in the house. He had none, so he made some. He steered the boy's anguished father to Adam's home and waited outside. He couldn't go in, but the father could.

The father attacked Adam, giving Mackey cause to enter the house and search it. Jeffrey Cole wasn't there. As it turned out, the suspect was innocent of any involvement in young Cole's disappearance. Still, he'd been seriously beaten by the boy's father.

Wyms called Mackey on it. He made light of it, saying that even though the suspect was innocent in this case, he was still a pedophile who deserved a beating.

That was the straw that tipped the scales. Seeking out Chief Bankston, she said that if the precinct captaincy offer was still open, she'd take the job.

```
Surveillance   Transcript:   110-21434   Location   ref:
FARM-7449
-------------------------------------------------------
Chief Bankston: So now you want the job?

Claudette Wyms: No, but I'd take it.

Bankston: You always communicate in riddles?

Wyms: I've kept my head down long enough. I don't like
what I'm seeing lately. So it's either do something
about it or quit. And I'm way too young to retire.
```

Gang Killing

Tragedy struck with the murder of Wyms's ex-husband, Jeff Franklin, who was sitting in a parked car with their grown daughter, Bonnie, when a stranger walked up to him and shot him dead.

He was the first casualty of the resurgent Johnnies gang. The Johnnies were an OG (Original Gangter) black street gang that had been pushed to the

sidelines by Latino gangs such as the Toros, Los Mags, and the Quintero mob. With Armadillo dead and the Latino gangs in disarray, the black gangs were astir, eager to reclaim their place in the street hierarchy.

In the past, when they were riding high, the Johnnies had instituted the custom of random killings of civilians on April Fools' Day. For each gang member that had died in the previous year, they would kill a citizen. Any citizen would do. Total strangers, chosen at random, would be shot dead by gang members appointed as this year's executioners. It was done to terrify others, to demonstrate their power and propensity for cold-blooded murder.

And to send a message to the other gangs, too.

Approaching an unsuspecting victim, the executioner would announce, "Johnny says April Fools'," and shoot the other dead.

Jeff Franklin was this year's first victim. Daughter Bonnie could identify the killer. This put Claudette Wyms in a quandary. She didn't want her daughter being a star witness in a gang killing. She shaped that part of the investigation so that Bonnie was shielded from being put in that position. In that effort, she was helped by her partner, Dutch Wagenbach.

The case was finally broken by Strike Team detectives Mackey and Garris.

Still, Claudette Wyms can't afford to relax her vigilance in protecting her daughter from possible gang reprisals.

```
Surveillance   Transcript:   655-55710   Location   ref:
FARM-9562
----------------------------------------------------------------
Claudette Wyms: Results don't excuse bad behavior.

Mackey: Tell you what. It's clear you and I have some
issues. So why don't we agree just not to work with
each other anymore?

Wyms: The question isn't whether I can work with you.
It's how you're going to handle working for me.
```

6. DETECTIVE HOLLAND "DUTCH" WAGENBACH

Surveillance Transcript: 029-25360 Location ref:
FARM-7979

Dutch Wagenbach: Who stole my Ding Dongs?

When he first started work at the Barn, Detective Holland "Dutch" Wagenbach was polite, soft-spoken, and considerate of the rights of his fellow officers. In the hard-charging Farm Division, that was a sure route toward getting tagged as the precinct "rube"—the goat, the nerdish butt of some raw cop humor.

The laughter stopped when Wagenbach started breaking some big cases.

He learned fast, too, learned to throw the abuse back in the faces of the other cops when they tried to set him up as a patsy.

Flying Dutchman

Wagenbach (pronounced "wagonbock") is divorced, with no kids. His ex-wife, Lucy, was a drunk who joined Alcoholics Anonymous, where she had an affair with her sponsor. She left Dutch and had the sponsor's baby.

Farmington File Photo: Jenny Reborg Case #369-C.

Wagenbach has been a member of the department for twelve years. All his previous partners spoke Spanish, so he never learned the language. He transferred out of Sunset Division into the Barn when it was being formed up.

Since he began working the Farm, he's been trying to master at least a few Spanish phrases. Recently he began taking classes in the language.

Dutch Wagenbach likes to try to get into a suspect's mind and try to psych him or her out. All detectives do this, to some extent. But Wagenbach's done some extensive studying in forensic psychology, trying to understand the criminal mind. Sometimes, too much theory gets in the way of his natural instincts and causes him to make some bad guesses. One of the worst was the Bob and Marcy Lindhoff case.

Other times, though, his hunches pay off, as when he broke the case of the Streetwalker Killer, a serial sex slayer who preyed on street hookers.

Ding Dongs

Wagenbach's advent at the Barn was not an auspicious one. On day one, he arrived late. At Sunset Division, starting time was nine a.m. At Farmington, it was seven a.m. As a result, he was two hours late for his first day of work. Captain Aceveda took notice and told him not to be late again.

All the good squad room desks had already been taken. When he left his workstation on one errand or another, he'd often return to find his chair missing.

The needling had begun.

Still, he had enough smarts and inventiveness to go along with Claudette Wyms's approach to dealing with Jesus Latigo, a ransom broker for kinap rings—and that approach broke the case. Impressed, Dutch asked if she wanted to partner with him.

She said yes, and Aceveda made it official.

Wyms and Wagenbach were a team.

Wagenbach got his first real taste of the Vic Mackey experience about four months into the job, during the Jenny Reborg case.

The girl's crackhead father had killed her mother and sold Jenny for $200 to a sexual deviant. The deviant liked young teen girls, not eight-year-olds like Jenny, so he'd traded her to Dr. Grady, a dominant sadistic pedophile he'd met on the Net.

Dutch interrogated Grady, who wouldn't crack. Within hours, Grady's lawyer would have him released. Then, if he managed to elude police surveillance, he could get to the girl he had hidden and do away with her.

Time was running out.

That was when Aceveda brought in Mackey. He went into the interrogation room where Grady was being held and emerged a short time later with the address of the locale where the girl was.

Jenny Reborg was saved.

• • •

During the case, Dutch had gotten a little full of himself. His knowledge of forensic psychology had given him a swelled head. He was a little too puffed up with himself, too cocky.

After the case was closed, he discovered that something in his desk stank. He didn't have to be a detective to find out what it was. A very big piece of dog crap had been left in one of his desk drawers.

It was an old cop custom: whenever somebody got too full of himself, he'd get taken down a peg by having some dog crap left in his desk.

Going to work with rubber gloves, wire brush, and industrial-strength cleaners and disinfectant, Wagenbach managed to detoxify his desk.

```
Surveillance   Transcript:   022-96944   Location   ref:
FARM-5103
--------------------------------------------------------------
Claudette Wyms (to Mackey): Fork over his Ding Dongs.
```

Earlier, he'd accused Vic Mackey of stealing the Ding Dong snack cakes that he'd stowed away for later, an accusation that Mackey denied.

Now he accused Mackey of perpetrating the desk-defiling dirty deed. Mackey laughed it off, announcing out loud for all the squad room to hear that he'd spare no effort to find the real culprit.

So far, though, the perpetrator's identity remains a mystery.

Still, it's worth noting that Dutch's partner, Claudette Wyms, is the owner of a very big dog.

```
Surveillance   Transcript:   009-83619   Location   ref:
FARM-5107
--------------------------------------------------------------
Dutch Wagenbach (on Vic Mackey): How come everybody
loves this asshole so much?
```

Jousting

Less humorous was a disturbing incident following Detective Terry Crowley's death. Without preamble or buildup, Aceveda asked Dutch to help him out with an interrogation. Wagenbach was surprised if not shocked to find out that the subject of the interview was a cop,

IAD surveillance caught Dutch hearing about having to team up with his new partner: Vendrell.

Detective Shane Vendrell.

Keeping Vendrell isolated in interrogation while Mackey was busy elsewhere, Aceveda grilled him about the circumstances of Terry Crowley's death, making him repeat his story several times, zeroing in on any inconsistencies.

Dutch entered into the spirit of the thing, mostly serving as a foil to Aceveda. As the interrogation progressed, Vendrell became sweaty and flustered.

Wagenbach said of Vendrell, "You notice how every time he lies he squints?"

Before the matter could be resolved, Mackey barged in and sent Vendrell on his way, ending the interview.

Wagenbach's next extended encounter with Vendrell was quite different. It came after IAD had ruled on Crowley's death, clearing the Strike Team, but during their investigation of alleged Strike Team drug thefts. The Strike Team was temporarily deactivated, its members partnered with detectives outside the squad.

Dutch was paired with Vendrell, working a year-old case that had fallen into the cracks after the retirement of the originally assigned sleuth, Detective Tom Gannon. The same Gannon who'd caught the Beechwood Canyon Slasher.

The case was the unsolved murder of Kyle Kelner, a local real estate businessman. The investigation had gone cold, with no leads.

Checking on the flight records of Kelner's former business partner, Ari, Wagenbach discovered that Ari had lied about his movements at the time of the murder, claiming to have been on a different flight from the one he'd actually taken. Confronted with his now defunct alibi, the ex-partner confessed to the murder. Motive: greed. He'd been stealing funds from the business.

Almost plaintively, he asked, "How come you guys didn't catch me last year?"

A happier by-product of the case was that it caused Dutch to meet the victim's widow, Kim Kelner. Womanizer Shane Vendrell was first to try to make a move on her, a ploy initially derided by Dutch. Later though, while trying to extend a professional courtesy to her, Dutch began dating Kim Kelner and the two ultimately entered into a romantic relationship.

The Streetwalker Strangler

A cop needs to be thick-skinned to keep from being overwhelmed by seeing the pain and suffering of so many other people.

To every cop, sooner or later, comes a case that can't be kept at arm's length, that sinks its barbs into the heart and soul and just won't let go, demanding to be solved, to let justice be done.

For Dutch Wagenbach, it was the case of a young teen hooker known only by the street name Sally Struthers, whose life was brutally snuffed out by the serial sex sadist known as the Streetwalker Strangler.

She was the fifth victim. Like the others, she was a street hooker who hung out on the corner to attract customers and serviced them in their cars. And like the others, she was raped and murdered—not necessarily in that order—then placed facedown on the ground.

It was the killer's signature style. Dutch theorized that he posed them facedown because it was part of the domination and control that he craved.

Probably he was impotent with females—at least the live ones.

There was something about the pathetic nature of Sally's short, tragic life and grisly death that haunted Wagenbach. It preyed on his mind, consuming his waking thoughts. The case went cold but not for him.

Months passed and he still wouldn't let it drop.

He was looking for something—something. . . .

● ● ●

Finally, he found it.

Patrol Unit 1-Tango-13, Officers Danny Sofer and Julien Lowe, discovered a man masturbating in an alley. He was Sean Taylor, a Pasadena car radio installer. He'd committed a lewd act in public but was otherwise clean, so the officers let him go with a warning.

Later, speaking of the incident at the station, they were overheard by Detective Wagenbach. He was struck by the location of the incident, in an alley two blocks away from where Sally's body had been found.

To Dutch, Taylor was a person of interest. He requested that Taylor come down to the station for an interview. Taylor complied.

During a lengthy interrogation, he and Wagenbach engaged in a battle of wills. Taylor may have thought that he was playing cat to Wagenbach's mouse as he berated the detective for being a failure, a "lowly civil servant," and an ineffectual loser.

```
Surveillance  Transcript:  091-59569  Location  ref:
FARM-2125
---------------------------------------------------------
Taylor (to Dutch): You're still the same lonely kid
from high school. And at the end of the day, when you
look in the mirror, you don't see the person you wish
you were--just the lowly civil servant you hoped
you'd never become.

Dutch: Truth is, Sean, I may not have been the most
popular guy in high school, but I got laid. More than
a few times. And I'm getting laid now, too. And guess
what? She's hot. And why I became a cop? It had noth-
ing to do with respect. I just like to solve puzzles.
```

While Taylor was boasting about his own cleverness, Wagenbach was busy behind the scenes. The owner of a green car with a broken rear taillight verified that the car had been in Taylor's shop on the night that Sally was seen by witnesses getting into such a vehicle—the last time anyone but her killer ever saw her alive.

Taking that evidence to a judge, Wagenbach secured search warrants for Taylor's home and for the home of his aunt. Since Taylor had cosigned the mortgage for his aunt's home, it fell within the provenance of a warrant. His home came up clean—but his aunt's house yielded a harvest of horror, with seventeen female corpses buried in the crawl space under the front porch.

Confronted with the discovery during his interrogation, Taylor realized that he was caught and switched gears. Instead of continuing to deny his guilt, he reveled in it, bragging about his murders.

Either way, he was caught. Persistence bordering on obsession on the part of Detective Wagenbach had resulted in the apprehension of a lethal and cunning serial killer.

And some much-needed peace for Dutch.

```
Surveillance  Transcript:  045-12024  Location  ref:
FARM-7540
-----------------------------------------------------------
Dutch: How typical you are. The moment you're caught,
you try to be special.

Taylor: I killed twenty-two people--twenty-three,
counting that "hunting accident." Oh, I'm special,
all right.

Dutch: If you're so special, how come a lowly civil
servant like me just caught you?
```

Hit-and-Run

During the 911 riots, Claudette Wyms's regular duties were set aside so she could appear with Captain Aceveda at various sites in the Grove, addressing the community, trying to keep the lid on the boiling pot of street unrest.

To Wagenbach alone, then, came the case of Anthony Nunez, killed by a hit-and-run driver in a blue Mercedes. It seemed routine, so Dutch was pleased and flattered when Vic Mackey approached him, offering to help out in the investigation.

Wagenbach welcomed the help. The Two Days of Blood killings and riots had stretched the division dangerously thin.

Mackey argued that the Nunez case was a toss and shoot—a gang-related killing in which the victim is thrown in front of an oncoming car to make the death look like an accident. Guns are then fired so the driver speeds on his way instead of getting out to investigate the damage.

Mackey noted that Nunez banged with the Toros, that he'd been out on the street selling drugs when he was struck. It looked like a gang kill, possibly by the rival Los Mags.

Dutch wasn't so sure. Doing some digging, he learned that the blue Merc had been seen around the neighborhood, parked outside the residence of one Sedona Tellez. His interest was further piqued by the discovery that Tellez had moved out of her apartment right after the accident.

Mackey's toss-and-shoot theory took on more substance with the discovery of the body of Jesus Rosales, Nunez's buddy and partner. Rosales had been shot dead through the heart, his corpse dumped under an overpass in Los Mags turf.

Dutch kept looking for Tellez anyway—and found her.

Farmington File Photo: Two Days of Blood Case #73-8A. Subject: Det. Wagenbach's interrogation techniques.

```
Surveillance   Transcript:   013-51395   Location   ref:
FARM-2097
----------------------------------------------------------

Mackey: You found all this out since four o'clock?

Dutch: Pretty good, huh?

Mackey: Too good, Dutch-boy.

Dutch: Well, I got a rep to maintain.

Mackey: You're gonna put me out of a job.
```

As it turned out, it was Assistant Chief Gilroy who was out of a job, arrested and charged with vehicular manslaughter and fraud. Sedona Tellez had worked in his office for several months. The married Gilroy fell for her hard. They cooked up a scheme to destabilize the Grove, buy up neighborhood properties when they were low, restabilize the area, and sell the properties to developers for big profits.

It was a hell of a bust.

Wagenbach was credited as being the chief detective on the Gilroy hit-and-run case.

Butterfly

The hard facts of life on the Farm were brought home to Dutch when he and Wyms first began jousting with Armadillo Quintero during the investigation of

the burning death of Cuca Reyes. The victim's family wouldn't talk, but Wagenbach sensed that twelve-year-old Mayda Reyes had something she wanted to tell. Concluding the interview at the family residence, he accidentally on purpose left his notebook behind.

As he'd guessed, the next day Mayda came to the station to return the notebook. He took her into an interrogation room for privacy. She told him that Armadillo had been "wooing" Cuca, trying to get him to join his gang.

At this point, Claudette Wyms learned of the visit. She ended the interview, telling Dutch that to use the girl as a witness in a gang case would put her in grave danger.

"If you had kids, you'd understand," she said. She took the girl home.

Several hours later, Armadillo was arrested on a charge of harboring a felon and brought to the Barn. A flimsy charge, but at least it was a pretext for bringing him in so the detectives could take the measure of the man.

Quintero was cool, self-contained, aware of his rights. By coincidence, he was placed in the same interrogation room that had earlier been occupied by Mayda. It was sheer chance, a freak fluke that he was put in this interrogation room and not one of the others.

At one point in the grilling, the detectives left the room, leaving Armadillo alone. Afterward, Dutch noticed that Armadillo had a new cockiness, a smugness that he hadn't had before.

He knew he hadn't imagined it; it was real and it nagged at him. Reviewing the videotapes from the camera that had been continuously monitoring the room, he and Wyms discovered that at one point while he was alone, Armadillo noticed something on the floor and picked it up.

This occurred immediately before his sudden attitude change.

Closer examination of the tape's magnified image revealed that the object found by Quintero was a butterfly hair clip that belonged to Mayda. It must have fallen off. Quintero took notice of it, and knew to whom it belonged. He'd been eyeing Mayda pretty closely—he liked young girls.

By the time Wyms and Wagenbach had made their discovery, Armadillo had already been released and out on the street for several hours. Time enough for him to abduct and rape the girl, and have the tattoo of a dove etched into her face, his signature.

He got away with it, too.

Bob and Marcy

In the matter of Bob and Marcy Lindhoff, Detective Wagenbach tripped over his own technique.

Dutch is pretty methodical at a crime scene.

It was a missing-person case that began with something being found—namely, a severed human hand and forearm. Some kids found it while playing in a yard.

The severed limb was that of an adult white female. It showed signs of having been taken from a living person. Fingerprints identified it as belonging to Kayla LeSeur, whose roommate stated that Kayla had been away from the apartment since the previous evening. Kayla had not been heard from since.

The way in which the arm had been amputated below the elbow indicated that some pains had been taken to keep from killing the victim. Kayla might still be alive.

Kayla's neighbors in the apartment next door were Bob and Marcy Lindhoff, a married couple. Marcy was in her early twenties; Bob was seventeen years older.

A search of the record revealed that nine years ago Bob Lindhoff had been arrested on a kidnapping complaint. He'd gone off on a trip with a young woman who was about the same age then as Marcy was now. She went with him without telling her parents. Assuming the worst, they'd notified the police.

Since the woman was over the legal age of consent, no charges were filed and Bob Lindhoff was released. He'd had a clean record ever since.

Still, there was something about Bob and Marcy that set off alarm bells in Dutch Wagenbach's head. He had a hunch that Bob had gotten to Kayla, based largely on what he perceived to be Bob's psychological profile: manipulative, sadistic, control freak. The weak link was Marcy, Dutch thought.

In the interrogation room, he went to work on her, trying to psych her out. Theorizing that she was Bob's submissive puppet, he played the role of controlling dominator, shouting, browbeating her, demanding that she talk. Marcy broke down and wept, but she continued to maintain Bob's and her innocence.

"I broke her," Wagenbach crowed to Claudette Wyms. He was certain that she was telling the truth, and the couple was released.

A police search of Kayla's apartment revealed a peephole that had been bored through the bathroom wall, allowing her to be spied on by those in the next apartment: Bob and Marcy.

College records showed Bob had had two years of medical school, giving him the knowledge of how to successfully amputate a limb.

Wagenbach had already ordered Bob and Marcy released. They'd been at large for several hours before an APB was put out on them. They were apprehended while driving in their car, the same car that had been parked in the Barn's visitor's parking lot during the hours the two had been in the station answering questions.

Inside the trunk was the dead body of Kayla LeSuer. The evidence showed she'd been alive when put in the trunk, but had died some time afterward, perhaps while the car had been parked in the police lot.

It was a big black eye for the Barn, and Dutch took the heat for it. He was the one who'd let the killer couple go free from police custody.

He blamed himself. All the time he thought he'd been playing Marcy, she'd been playing him.

Worse, if Bob was to be believed, it had been Marcy's idea to cut off Kayla's arm.

Later, Marcy plea-bargained her way into an eight-year prison term, compared to Bob's life sentence. Part of her plea was that she couldn't lie about the crime, or the deal would collapse.

Dutch questioned her. He had to know.

She said that for a while Bob had been eyeing neighbor Kayla, wanting to work her into a threesome with him and Marcy. Marcy broached the idea to her, but

Kayla wanted none of it. Marcy lured her into the apartment, and then they had her.

According to Marcy, Bob had been talking about Kayla, obsessing about her, always saying how pretty he thought she was. Marcy had him amputate Kayla's arm below the elbow.

"She wasn't so pretty after that," Marcy said, shrugging.

The case got to Wagenbach. His confidence in his hunches and instincts took a big hit. It took some time for him to get his game back.

The turning point was the Leah Madson rape-murder case. She was young, obese. She'd been raped and strangled with her own bra straps. Chocolate stains on her fingertips indicated that shortly before being killed she'd been eating a candy bar.

The prime suspect was Stu Kleinsausser. He'd been out on a date with the victim the same night she was murdered. He denied any involvement in the crime, claiming she wasn't his type. He claimed he'd dropped her off early in the evening and hadn't seen her after that.

He was obese, isolated, unsocialized. Dutch's instincts told him that this was the killer, but the suspect wouldn't crack. There was no hard evidence, nothing that would hold up in court.

Dutch gave it one last shot,

Farmington File Photo: Two days of Blood Case #73-8A. Subject: Det. Wagenbach's interrogation techniques.

returning to the interrogation room for another crack at the suspect. This time he poured it on, breezing along, acting as if he all but had the conviction in his hip pocket.

He told Kleinsausser that he was sunk, that police searchers had found the dead woman's missing bra clasp in his car.

The suspect cracked, babbling out a confession while trying to flatten Dutch. He didn't know that the police hadn't found the missing bra clasp in his car or anywhere else. It was all a bluff to catch a killer.

Dutch Wagenbach was back in the groove.

Well, not entirely. There were still those miscues, those awkward social gaffes. Like the time he hired an illegal immigrant, a material witness in a case of negligent homicide, to fix a retaining wall on his property.

Or during the investigation of the shooting of a meter maid, when he was doing some sleuthing at the Traffic Violations Bureau and tried and failed to get a parking ticket fixed.

Or when he hit on Lanie Kellis—who cut him off at the knees.

He showed better form while probing the murder of Jeff Franklin, ex-husband of Claudette Wyms. He worked with Claudette to protect her daughter Bonnie from being identified as a prime witness in the gang-related killing.

The hard lesson of Mayda Reyes had taught him that the law has to be tempered with common sense.

He's always learning.

That's one of the things that makes him a good—and potentially great—detective.

7. PARTNERS: OFFICER DANIELLE SOFER AND OFFICER JULIEN LOWE

```
Surveillance   Transcript:   051-20043   Location   ref:
FARM-3513
---------------------------------------------------------------
Julien Lowe: What do you do when the man that you are
isn't the man you want to be?
```

Blues for Two

No good deed goes unpunished.

That cynical maxim unfortunately seems to apply to the hard luck and cruel twists of fate that have plagued uniformed cops Danielle "Danny" Sofer and Julien Lowe. Partners on the street, both have suffered personally and professionally simply because they've chosen to wear the badge and the gun.

Danny Sofer is single. At the time of the Barn start-up, she held a P2 (Patrol Second) rank. She was involved in an ongoing affair with married man Vic Mackey. She was selected to be the Training Officer of rookie officer Julien Lowe.

Julien Lowe is now married with a ten-year-old stepson. At the time he began at the Barn, he was single. A lifelong resident of the Farmington district, Lowe has stated that he joined the force "to make a difference." He is devoutly religious, a regular churchgoer and a member of various prayer groups.

By a strange combination of circumstances, from the beginning Danny Sofer and Julien Lowe have been involved in some of the pivotal events affecting the division. They were present for the Strike Team's first big bust, when dealer Lionel Phipps's place was raided for drugs. In fact, it was Julien who found a cache of crack cocaine hidden in the bathroom.

They were there during the Ara's Pastry drug bust, with its aftermath of alleged drug thefts by the Strike Team.

They were the second unit at the scene in response to the phony 911 call that set up the first ambush murders of police officers.

Danny Sofer was the arresting officer who put Pinto in the holding pen, where he produced a hidden knife that he used to kill Armadillo Quintero.

They've both paid a heavy price for their dedicated police work.

Internal Affairs

Danny Sofer and Julien Lowe were among the backup units during the Strike Team's bust of the Armenian mob's Ara's Pastry drug-dealing site.

After the raid, Lowe went to see Captain Aceveda. He said that after much soul-searching, he'd decided it was his duty to report something he'd seen during the bust.

Strike Team members Mackey, Vendrell, and Lemansky were alone in the bakery kitchen. Julien had been standing outside the kitchen, where he could see them but they couldn't see him and didn't know he was there. Mackey took two bricks of cocaine from the drug stash and gave them to Vendrell, who stuffed them in his weapons bag and left the premises.

Aceveda carefully asked Julien Lowe if he wanted to stand by his statement. He cautioned him that he was making a serious charge. Also, by breaking the so-called Blue Wall of Silence, the unspoken pact by which cops are forbidden to testify against other cops, Julien would be exposing himself to potential hostility from his coworkers.

Even honest cops generally dislike those who inform against dirty cops. They feel the informant can't be trusted. Withdrawing that trust can leave the officer who came forward with the truth in a lonely position, exposed in no-man's-land. He may not be able to rely on other officers covering his back.

Farmington File Photo: Case #9-D.
Subject: Offcs. Danielle Sofer
and Julien Lowe on patrol.

Julien Lowe said he was aware of these things, but that his conscience wouldn't let him keep quiet about what he'd seen.

Aceveda must have been quietly thrilled. Since the death of Terry Crowley (and even before), he'd been itching to get something on Mackey. He was sure Mackey was dirty—guilty of murdering Crowley and much else.

Julien signed a statement, and Aceveda submitted it to IAD, which opened an investigation. The probe was supposed to be confidential, but once the IAD sleuths came around to the Barn asking questions, word of their real purpose leaked out.

It was news to Danny Sofer. She'd been unaware of what Julien claimed to have seen, and that he'd taken it to Aceveda. When she found out, she didn't like it.

First of all, she told Julien that he must be mistaken, that Vic Mackey wasn't the kind of guy to steal drugs. She was angry that he hadn't told her of his decision to go to the captain.

Partnership is about trust, she said. Partners have got to level with each other. If they don't, it tears down trust and can ultimately lead to disaster for themselves and/or others.

Julien acknowledged what she was saying, but it didn't change his mind. He knew that Danny and Mackey were more than just friends, and that their relationship might well affect her judgment about the "real" Vic.

Julien Lowe had forgotten the saying about those who live in glass houses. On the street, he was professional, in control. In private, his life was out of control. He was conflicted—sexually conflicted.

According to Tomas Motyashik, he and Julien had a sexual relationship. Bear in mind, too, that Motyashik has a lengthy record of petty crime and, as will be seen below, has reasons for wishing to do Julien harm.

Tomas says that Julien was tormented by what he called his "urges"—his sexual attraction to other men. Julien denied rumors that he was gay. But he had these urges. It was doubly tormenting for him, because he was a genuinely religious man. To him, homosexuality was not an alternate lifestyle—it was a sin.

Before meeting Tomas, Julien had yet to act on these urges.

Doubting Tomas

During an open-warrants sweep, where precinct police comb the district for fugitives with outstanding arrest warrants on them, one of those arrested was Tomas Motyashik.

He was a small-time crook, penny-ante scam

Sofer and Lowe seem to make a good team—despite their differences.

artist, and part-time male hustler. Though not without a certain glib charm. And why not? After all, charming people so he could get something out of them was part of his stock in trade.

He'd been picked up on a bad-check rap. While in a holding cell, he maintained to all who would listen that the warrant was a clerical mistake, that the bad-check charges against him had already been dismissed.

Checking on his claim, Julien Lowe discovered that Tomas was right, that the charges had been dropped and the arrest was a mistake. Thanks to his efforts, Tomas was released.

Striking up a conversation, Tomas told Julien that he looked familiar. Hadn't he seen Julien hanging around outside the Abbey, in West Hollywood?

The Abbey is a gay club.

Julien said Tomas must be mistaking him for someone else. Leaving, Tomas invited Julien to visit him at the apartment where he was staying. Later, while off duty, Julien did just that.

They began a sexual relationship. Julien, more tormented than ever, continued to insist, "I'm not gay," even as he continued seeing Tomas. He had more to worry about than the state of his soul. There was a deadly real practical matter involved.

Julien was deeply closeted.

Julien was a cop.

Shame and guilt were anchored by the very real fear of his homosexuality being revealed to his fellow officers.

Policing is essentially a macho culture, with little tolerance for alternate sexual lifestyles. Exposure could make his life a living hell. In an aggressive, almost paramilitary division like Farmington, there were no openly gay officers. If they were gay, they kept it to themselves and prayed it wouldn't get out.

As did Julien.

But Julien Lowe had now crossed paths with Vic Mackey. Worse, he'd threatened Mackey. His charge about the drug theft had put Mackey and

Vendrell in danger. Whatever the truth of the charges, Mackey wasn't about to just sit back and let Julien's testimony bounce him off the force and maybe even into jail.

Tomas Motyashik says that around this time Mackey showed up at the apartment where he was staying to serve him with an arrest warrant. According to Tomas, Mackey found him in bed with Julien.

Again, we have here only the words of Tomas to go by. Mackey and Julien aren't talking. But it's a matter of record that, during the time period in question, Mackey did apprehend Tomas and bring him into the Barn.

People make mistakes, Mackey said. Julien had been mistaken in what he thought he'd seen in the bakery kitchen. Now he had to admit that "mistake" and get on with his life.

Tomas Motyashik was released. He made himself scarce and Julien didn't see him anymore.

At about the same time, Julien went to Aceveda to retract his statement. He said he'd done a lot of thinking about the matter, and the more he thought about it, the less sure he was that he'd seen what he thought he'd seen.

He couldn't swear to it that Mackey had taken two bricks of cocaine. They might have been boxes of ammo, as Mackey and Vendrell maintained in their statements to IAD investigators.

Aceveda was coldly furious. He knew that Mackey had somehow gotten to Julien. With Julien dropping his statement, the IAD investigation was dead—as dead as Terry Crowley.

As a result of his withdrawing the charges, and without protest on his part, Officer Julien Lowe was sentenced by Captain Aceveda to be fined a week's pay and put on probation for a period of thirty (30) days.

Bite Marks

Police work demands trust. In the aftermath of the IAD drug probe, trust was lacking in the Sofer-Lowe pairing. Julien distrusted Danny Sofer because of her closeness to Mackey, while she distrusted him because of his tight-lipped, loner ways.

Around this time, both Danny and Julien separately approached Aceveda, requesting that he assign them new partners. Aceveda refused those requests.

For a time, the partnership hit a rough patch, marked on both sides by hostility, resentment, and open quarreling.

Then Danny Sofer was attacked and bitten by a male street hooker with AIDS.

Frank, 22, a ravaged black drag queen, was arrested and brought to the Barn. He resisted being put in a holding cell, repeatedly shrieking, "I can't go in there!"

"You should've thought about that before you solicited a cop," Officer Sofer said offhandedly.

The prisoner lunged at her, taking her by surprise, knocking her down and biting her on the arm.

Julien began beating him with his nightstick. This caused the attacker's blood to fly, doubly dangerous because Danny had open wounds from the bite.

Danny's attacker was revealed to be HIV positive. Under questioning, he stated that he had gotten AIDS in jail, that he bit Danny because he wanted to infect her.

While it is generally held that AIDS cannot be transmitted by biting, nobody wants to be a test case to find out. Barn personnel were mindful of the haunting fate of one of their own, an officer who was pricked by a contaminated needle during a search and contracted AIDS.

Later, while being transferred from the Barn holding cell to Central, the biter sustained serious injuries that required immediate hospitalization and emergency treatment.

IAD Surveillance Photo: #103-C.
Subject: Patrol apprehension
technique.

His condition was critical. Apparently he'd slipped and fallen while getting into the police van, causing his injuries.

That was the official version.

The prisoner, who later recovered, claimed that while he was in the van a blanket was thrown over his head and he was beaten by police.

This is not unlikely. He'd attacked a police officer in front of other prisoners in the holding cell. In the eyes of the Barn, he was guilty.

The sentence was swift punishment, served up in the form of a blanket party. A blanket was thrown on his head so he couldn't see his assailants to identify them. He was then beaten with nightsticks. Clubbed.

Unofficially, the Barn rumor mill and grapevine hold that the beating was the work of Officers Paul Jackson, Ray Carlson, and Julien Lowe. Jackson and Carlson were uniformed patrol officers with a record of disciplinary infractions. A couple of bad apples. According to the unwritten code of the squad room, as Danny Sofer's partner, Julien would be expected to be the one to deliver the beating—a cruel irony, in light of later events.

Of course, this is pure hearsay, totally inadmissible as evidence. Officially, there was no beating.

● ● ●

Danny Sofer returned to duty with a clean bill of health. She knew the truth about the blanket party and didn't like it. She hadn't wanted the prisoner to be beaten within an inch of his life.

She told Julien, "All the problems we've had, I thought the one thing I could count on was you had a good heart."

The hostility and mutual resentment between them was gone. But Julien was still at war with himself, perhaps now more than ever.

He and Danny were dispatched to the site of a graduation party. The party had been crashed by an angry ex-boyfriend with a gun. Shots were fired; fortunately no one was hurt.

When the officers arrived, the gunman fled, pursued on foot by Julien Lowe. Cornering him, Julien persuaded the youth to give up his gun and surrender peacefully.

It was an act of conspicuous bravery. Aceveda told Lowe that he might well be up for a commendation.

Danny Sofer had a different view. She knew that Julien had kept his gun holstered while apprehending the armed teen. Moreover, he hadn't been wearing his protective Kevlar vest.

She asked, "Did you want to get shot? Julien, did you want to die?" She asked if it was because he was gay.

He was shocked by what she'd said.

She told him that partners can't keep secrets from each other.

Julien decided to seek solace through his church. To his clergyman, Reverend Neal Cook, he confessed his gay "urges" and how he prayed for the strength to "beat them down."

The reverend told him of an outreach program that the church was conducting. It was a sexual reorientation therapy group that met every Thursday. It was for men like him, who had "urges" but wanted to overcome them. It treated homosexuality as an "addiction," like alcoholism and drug taking.

It was a support group that used prayer and counseling to reorient its members toward heterosexuality, to "reprogram them with God's help."

Julien threw himself into the effort. It gave him ease, the ability to be at peace with himself.

The Shooting

Danny Sofer had the blahs. Her life felt like it was in a holding pattern. Her affair with Mackey was going nowhere. Maybe that was how she wanted it. Or maybe she should just break up with him and move on.

She was lonely. The loneliness of a woman in a macho male cop's world. For a while, Dutch Wagenbach had a crush on her. She was studying for the sergeant's exam, which he'd passed. He offered to help her study for it. They had some study dates. For her, it was more about studying than dating. Dutch was nice, but it wasn't going any further than that.

Around this time, a very bizarre incident seemed to encapsulate Danny's malaise. It occurred while she and Julien were detailed to protect a Korean-American minister who'd made enemies by denouncing street gang violence from the pulpit. While on duty, Danny noticed a guy around her age helping a child bury something in the ground.

Going to investigate, she learned that the man was helping the child bury a dead squirrel. They were giving the animal a funeral, complete with a tiny grave marked by a tiny cross. Danny was touched by the situation; taking the time to help out a child that way seemed like a sweet thing for a grown man to do.

The guy was about her own age and kind of cute, as she later told some of her female coworkers. Danny was intrigued and left the scene feeling better.

A few days later, though, Danny noticed the same man buying something from another child. He was buying more dead small animals, road kill and the like, so he could bury them. On a plot of land, he had a mass graveyard of dead and buried varmints. Apparently he had a bizarre kink for the fetishized burial of small dead things.

It was too weird. Danny wasn't sure if he'd even violated a law, but she gave him a warning to cease and desist his funerary activities anyway. It was just one more example of street weirdness to share with her colleagues so they could shake their heads in wonder at some of the characters out there in the district.

Danny didn't know it, but her world was about to change. And not for the better.

A woman called the Barn desk to complain that her neighbor was a terrorist. It sounded like a crank call, but in the anxious post-9/11 climate, someone had to check it out. Unit 1-Tango-13 was dispatched to investigate.

The complainant was Alene, a single mother with several children who lived in an apartment complex. She said that her next-door neighbor was a terrorist and that he was cooking up something inside his apartment—probably some biological or chemical terror weapon.

The neighbor was Zayed Al-Thani, a Syrian immigrant who'd been living in the United States for five years. He was married. His pregnant wife, Yahssirah, was present in the apartment.

Danny Sofer asked if she and Julien could take a look inside the apartment. Zayed said no, standing on his constitutional right not to let them in. Danny said that in that case she'd have to pass the complaint along to the FBI, who'd follow it up. Al-Thani reluctantly allowed them into the apartment.

There was nothing suspicious. The smell about which the neighbor had complained was merely that of some food cooking in the kitchen.

Danny politely thanked the Al-Thanis, apologizing for the intrusion but explaining how it was their job to investigate. Zayed, bitter, said it was an example of anti-Arab bias.

Within a week, the officers were called back to the scene. This time, it was Zayed Al-Thani who'd called in a complaint, reporting that while his prayer rug was hanging out to dry on a line, his neighbor Alene's dog had chewed it up.

Alene, the same woman who'd called in the terrorist complaint, was also outside, loudly arguing her version of events.

They were both given a verbal warning by Lowe, who told them to go into their homes and stay away from each other.

Reports of a disturbance at the apartment complex brought Sofer and Lowe back to the site for a third visit, this time at night. Zayed Al-Thani and Alene were outside in front of the building, having a shouting match.

The inciting incident this time was that Alene had hung a large American flag off a balcony so that it fell across the Al-Thanis' front window, blocking it.

Now Zayed tore down the flag, tossing it to the ground. Alene went into her apartment, emerging with a kitchen knife. She was disarmed and subdued by Julien Lowe. He took her back into her apartment.

In the meantime, Zayed Al-Thani had drawn a handgun and was waving it around. Her own gun drawn and leveled, Danny Sofer shouted repeated commands for him to drop the weapon.

He would not. Highly agitated, wild-eyed, shouting, he flailed about with the gun, acting in so wild and uncontrolled a manner that Danny was in fear for her life.

After he disregarded her final warning, she fired, killing him.

• • •

As per department policy in such cases, Danny was given two days off for mandatory downtime. Also according to routine policy, an IAD investigation was opened into the shooting.

A setback appeared when Julien told IAD investigators that he hadn't seen the shooting. He'd been in the apartment arresting Alene.

IAD Surveillance Photo: #84-E. Subject: Offcr. Sofer discharging weapon.

There was a lot of feeling around the precinct that Julien should have said he'd seen the shooting even if he hadn't, to back up his partner. Danny herself couldn't help but resent it.

Things got worse. Although she'd failed the sergeant's exam, missing the passing grade by only three points, she was also in line for a promotion. It was her turn. She'd earned it. Her name was at the top of the list of candidates for promotion.

She didn't get it. The next name on the list after hers did. Aceveda explained that it was because of the shooting investigation and because of questions raised about her behavior in the aftermath (see below).

Fresh woes followed, in the form of a $5 million lawsuit being filed by the lawyer of the widowed Yahssirah Al-Thani. It accused the police department of causing Zayed Al-Thani's wrongful death, anti-Arab prejudice, violation of constitutional rights, etc.

Foremost in the list of those cited as defendants was Officer Danny Sofer. Right behind her was Captain David Aceveda.

The piling on continued as a man named Abu Ibish filed a complaint alleging that some months earlier, while investigating an incident at the Lakeside Tavern, Officer Sofer had addressed him with vicious anti-Arab slurs.

Probing the charge, Aceveda questioned Julien Lowe, who remembered the incident. The charges were untrue, he said. Danny Sofer had treated Ibish with every professional courtesy. What's more, at the time Ibish had made some bigoted antiblack remarks toward Julien.

That tossed it back to Ibish. Under questioning, he admitted that he'd been paid by the widow Al-Thani's lawyer to make the false charges. It was his word against the lawyer's, who was safe from being charged.

However, the $5 million lawsuit against the precinct was dead. In a dramatic station house encounter, Mrs. Al-Thani confronted Danny, shouting, "Justice will find you!"

Soon after, Danny Sofer began being harassed by a person or persons unknown. While parked outside her apartment in the Hollywood Division, her car was doused with yellow paint.

Someone called the Barn and falsely reported that Danny's mother had been killed in an auto accident.

She reported the pattern of harassment, but Aceveda could do nothing. She was sure that Yahssirah Al-Thani was behind it, but there was no proof.

The destabilization of Danny Sofer continued one day at work when she was approached by a pair of IAD detectives. They said they'd received an anonymous tip that she was dealing drugs out of her patrol car.

She indignantly denied the charge, saying it was all part of the pattern of harassment she'd been experiencing lately. Documented harassment, on the record.

They searched her patrol vehicle anyway and found a bag of marijuana. Danny said the drugs had been planted.

It was noted that the car had been left standing unlocked in the Barn parking lot, which was unguarded, affording plenty of opportunity for anyone who wanted to plant false evidence.

Danny's fingerprints were not found on the bag, and IAD cleared her.

Rattled, not thinking straight, Danny made the mistake of calling Yahssirah Al-Thani at home, accusing her of the harassment and demanding that she stop.

Aceveda ordered her to publicly apologize to the widow for making the call. This was done in Aceveda's office in the presence of the widow and her lawyer.

Lowe Pressure Zone

While Danny's life seemed to be coming apart, Julien Lowe was starting to feel that his life was getting back on track. He was sticking with the sexual re-orientation therapy group. Prayer seemed to be helping.

Through his job, he met Vanessa. She was a single mom trying to make a living and raise her ten-year-old son, Randall. She was religious, a regular churchgoer.

Randall was caught shoplifting spray-paint cans from a store and brought to the Barn, where his mother was called and told to come get him.

Vanessa and Julien struck up a conversation. She said how hard it was for a single mother to raise a boy to resist the temptations of the street, even with the help of her church. Julien sympathized. He gave Randall a stern lecture to throw a scare of lawbreaking into him.

He asked Vanessa out on a date. A whirlwind courtship followed. Within a few months, Julien had proposed marriage to her and she'd accepted.

He invited Danny to attend the upcoming wedding. She appeared to have reservations about going, and for a time, there was a notable coolness between her and Julien. It's possible that, if she believed he was gay, she might have thought he was making a big mistake entering into a heterosexual marriage—but this is only conjecture.

In any case, she did attend the wedding.

Negligent Homicide

Danny Sofer didn't want to arrest Pinto, even though he was walking down the middle of the sidewalk in broad daylight smoking a marijuana joint. Didn't want to arrest him, because it was a Mickey Mouse bust, a nothing,

Sofer's tenacious—and it sometimes gets her into trouble.

not even worth the paperwork needed to process it. Not with so many other real crimes going down on the Farm.

But Pinto had to push it. Instead of getting rid of the joint and going on his way like the officers told him to, he blew smoke in Danny's face. So she arrested him and brought him to the Barn.

Later, when Danny thought the bust over, she would come to the conclusion that Pinto had wanted to be arrested.

Danny gave him a thorough search, as she'd done before to hundreds of arrestees. The search revealed no weapons or contraband. Pinto was then put in the holding cell. Not long after, he produced a knife and stabbed Armadillo Quintero to death.

The killing made the Barn look bad, with departmental brass, the press, and the public.

Danny took the heat for the slaying. Her alleged negligence had allowed Pinto to sneak a knife into the cell and commit murder.

She claimed the charge was bogus. She'd searched him and he hadn't had any weapons. But if he hadn't sneaked the knife past her, how had he gotten the weapon?

From another prisoner?

Or from a cop? Maybe another Strike Team cop?

Danny said she didn't believe it. But she believed it enough to seek out Vic Mackey for an angry confrontation. She said that he was always talking about being a stand-up guy. Well, he knew that it wasn't through any fault of hers that Pinto had gotten a knife in the holding cell.

If he was a stand-up guy, as he liked to boast, how about standing up for her now? Or was he just going to keep quiet and let her take the rap?

Mackey had nothing to say.

Danny knew she was on her own. She was expendable.

Inside Out

Out of the blue, Tomas Motyashik came back into Julien's life. He was in the Barn holding cell, under arrest for stealing some CDs from a store. With his record of prior arrests, he could wind up doing time.

Tomas says that Julien didn't want to know him anymore. Not the way Tomas wanted. That part of Julien's life was over. He was married now, with a ten-year-old stepson.

That didn't faze Tomas. He'd been with lots of married guys with families. Julien repeated the message: they were through. Tomas accused Julien of abandoning him. He said that Mackey had told him to get lost and not contact Julien again.

Julien arranged for Tomas to be released. He got him settled in a motel room and lent him his credit card. Big mistake. Tomas charged up a bunch of stuff until the credit card company turned off the credit.

He put on some pressure, coming around to the station, hinting he was going to out Julien.

He wouldn't take no for an answer.

The next time they met, Julien brought along Gary Parsons, one of his friends from the Thursday-night church Sexual Reorientation Therapy group. Tomas later said that Julien had brought Gary along for moral support, to intervene with Tomas and convince him that Julien's past life was just that, past.

Tomas slugged Gary and fled. Gary's vision was damaged in one eye. He told police that he hadn't seen who struck him and couldn't identify him.

Julien wasn't going to put Gary in the position of lying to get him off the hook. He did what he had to do. He said that he'd seen the assault and identified Tomas as the culprit.

Tomas was apprehended and brought to the Barn, where, before a crowded station house, he screamingly denounced Julien for being a closeted gay.

• • •

That was when the treatment began.

The ringleaders were Jackson and Carlson, the ones who'd allegedly roped Julien into the alleged blanket party for the guy who bit Danny. Vicious and scurrilous flyers trashing Julien appeared on the bulletin board. Anonymous hate phone calls came to his house, saying ugly things about him to Vanessa and even to Randall.

Mackey approached him, saying that most of the precinct was for Julien and that the trouble was coming from only a few of the Barn jackasses.

As he'd promised, he'd kept Julien's secret. Several times, he'd reached out with friendly gestures, offering Julien basketball tickets (Julien was a Clippers fan), trying to sign him up for the Barn softball team. Julien had spurned the overtures. He figured Mackey was no friend.

Danny Sofer went to Aceveda and reported that Jackson and Carlson were behind the harassment. By now she was something of an expert on harassment herself.

It was a help to Aceveda. He was wrestling with Chief Bankston's demand that he cut 20 percent of the Barn's workforce. He recommended that Jackson and Carlson be fired from the department "with cause."

They were.

Unfortunately, he could do nothing to protect Danny Sofer from the same fate. On the eve of primary election day, she, too, received her notice of termination of employment. Aceveda had wanted to keep her, but the word had come down from the top that she had to go.

So there she was, through no fault of her own, out of a job.

Terminated.

She and Julien had a painful parting. He told her that he'd miss her, that she'd taught him what he knew about good police work. She had a warning for him: "Watch your back around these people."

But there was nothing she could do to protect him from a sudden, savage attack.

A day later, after dark, Julien went to take out the garbage at his home. A blanket was tossed over his head and four assailants started beating him.

Julien Lowe was brutally, bloodily beaten into unconsciousness—by police nightsticks.

The extent of his injuries has yet to be determined, but they're known to be serious. Perhaps critical.

Sometimes, Julien Lowe and Danny Sofer must feel like two of the loneliest people on the planet.

The Barn has busted many bad people. Here's a quick survey of some of the best of the worst:

Two-Time

Two-Time was a drug dealer in the district, a rival to Rondell Robinson. Unlike Rondell, Two-Time wasn't being protected by a dirty cop.

Mackey's informant, hooker Connie Riesler, told him that Two-Time had ordered up four of her pimp's "best girls" (she wasn't one of them) for an upcoming party. Party time meant that Two-Time would have plenty of drugs on the premises.

A judge issued a warrant and the Strike Team made ready for a night raid. For Detective Terry Crowley, it would be the first raid he'd make with the team.

They hit Two-Time's place at night, breaking in. The dealer fled to the bathroom, gun in hand, trying to flush the evidence down the toilet. He opened fire, shooting twice, downing Crowley.

Mackey and Vendrell returned fire, killing Two-Time.

That's the official version.

Dr. Bernard Grady

According to Dutch Wagenbach, Dr. Bernard Grady was a domination-control pedophile and sociopath. Grady acquired Jenny Reborg, 8, from George Sawyer, a deviant he'd met on the Internet.

Grady was brought into the Barn for questioning. Detectives were sure he had the girl hidden away at a secret location, but Grady wouldn't crack. Aceveda called in a specialist of his own: Vic Mackey.

Mackey was alone with Grady in an interrogation room. When he came out, he had the address where the girl was hidden. Jenny Reborg was saved.

Dr. Grady's attorney has since filed a complaint alleging that his client was brutalized and intimidated into confessing by police officers. Grady specifically identified Detective Mackey as the person who'd beaten a confession out of him.

However, a medical examination performed within hours of Grady's arrest found that he'd suffered no serious physical injury. A few bruises, which proved nothing. He might have had them when he came in.

Baby Banger Olman

A park food vendor was shot and seriously wounded. Wyms and Wagenbach caught the case. Initial suspicion fell on one Marlon Demeral, who'd been extorting money from park vendors in a "protection" shakedown racket. Demeral stated to detectives that within the previous six months he'd been driven out of the business by an up-and-coming Latino street gang, Los Magnificos—aka Los Mags.

Investigation revealed that the real shooter was Olman, a youngster just barely in his early teens.

He was old enough to pull a trigger. He'd already racked up a lengthy record of petty crime. Olman was a "baby banger," an aspiring gangbanger. He ran with

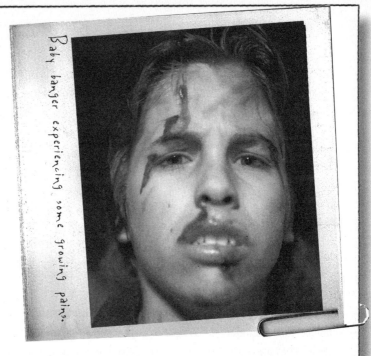

Baby banger experiencing some growing pains.

the junior auxiliary of Los Mags. He wanted to make the jump to the big leagues.

His entry into the Life was the shooting of the vendor, who'd refused to pay protection money to Los Mags. Olman thought he'd killed him and was proud of his work, his passport into the gang.

As an initiation rite, he was given a beating by the gang members. He had to take it to show how tough he was. Afterward, the big bangers welcomed him as one of their own.

At this point, the Strike Team raided the group, apprehending Olman.

As a minor, he could only be interviewed with the consent and in the presence of a parent or guardian, in this case his mother. She was present while Claudette Wyms interviewed Olman.

Wyms played him. He was so proud of having blasted his way into Los Mags. Wyms told him that the vendor was dead (not true) and that Demeral was taking the credit for the kill (also not true).

Furious, his pride stung, Olman said that he was the real killer.

Which was an admission of guilt.

Olman professed no fear at the idea of going to jail. He said he would be among family: Los Mags.

The Streetwalker Strangler

Sean Taylor, the streetwalker strangler, was originally from Chicago. When he was a kid, both his parents died in a fire. He was raised by an aunt. He scored high on intelligence tests and had good grades throughout school.

While he was in high school, on a hunting trip with a buddy, his friend was killed.

After college, Taylor worked at a car and truck stereo installation shop. He was single, a loner, with no close friends or acquaintances of either sex.

He was a sexual sadist, a predatory serial killer. Street hookers were his prey.

He incorporated his job into his extracurricular activities, using different cars that had been left overnight at the shop whenever he went out on the murder prowl. This allowed a constant changeover of vehicles, keeping the police from getting a fix on any one particular car as the killer's.

He always returned the vehicles to the owners cleaner than they'd been before the customers took them into the shop—cleaner because he'd painstakingly removed all traces of his crimes. That should've been a dead giveaway right there.

Cruising the nightscape, Taylor would lure street hookers into his car by pretending to be a john. He would then strangle them and do whatever it was he felt like doing to them. When he dumped the bodies, he would pose them facedown. He killed five that way.

But seventeen more victims were buried in the crawl space beneath his aunt's house. He'd run out of space—that was why he began dumping bodies on the street, in alleys and vacant lots.

That was what finally alerted the police to the presence of a serial killer working the streets of Farmington.

After being apprehended, he admitted to twenty-three homicides.

T-Bonz

T-Bonz was Salieri to Kern Little's Mozart. Envy was his ruling chord. Both homies were drug dealers turned hip-hop record producers. But Little had hits and stars while T-Bonz remained stuck in the minor leagues.

T-Bonz thought his ticket to the top would be rap artist Tyesha, who was also his girlfriend. He claimed to have "discovered" her. When she transferred her affections (and contract) to Little, T-Bonz took it hard.

He felt dissed.

Little threw a private party at the Shake Club to celebrate the release of Tyesha's new CD. T-Bonz and some of his thuggish crew crashed the festivities. He demanded the ridiculous sum of $2 million from Little for stealing Tyesha away.

The followers of T-Bonz and Little got in one another's faces. Shooting broke out, leaving four dead but the principals unharmed.

It didn't help that present on the scene were Danny Sofer and Curtis Lemansky, who were moonlighting as private security for the event.

A gang war was brewing between T-Bonz's crew and Little's crew. Soon after, a street clash between the two factions left four more corpses. Also killed in the fracas was an innocent young boy.

Mackey shuttled between the two sides, imposing a truce. Just when things seemed to have cooled down, Tyesha's dog was fed poisoned meat and died. She and Little both believed it was T-Bonz's handiwork.

Soon after, T-Bonz disappeared and has yet to resurface. Word on the street is that he's dead.

A story persists that, fed up with the carnage, Mackey decided to settle it by picking up T-Bonz and Little and locking them into an empty box container some- where near the river, leaving them there overnight.

The next morn- ing, when the door was opened, only Little came out. T-Bonz was dead, killed by Little with his bare hands.

"I always said he was a bitch," Little is quoted as saying. Some of his crew then went to work and made T-Bonz's body disappear.

That's the story on the street.

Margos Dezirian

Margos was an Armenian gang boss with international connection. He was one of those arrested as a result of the Ara's Pastry drug bust. Before the raid went down, Margos casually killed one of his associates, shooting him in the head.

The other two men arrested at the scene later professed ignorance as to Margos's reason for the shooting, which had taken them by surprise (to put it mildly). However, they also professed ignorance about anything relating to Margos, whom they obviously feared.

Before the killing, Margos had been cutting up some lines of cocaine. The associate helped himself to it, snorting the drug. Margos possibly took this as a mark of disrespect and summarily executed the other as punishment. However, this is only a theory.

A probe into his background indicated that Margos had extensive high-level crime connections in Eastern Europe and the Balkans. Recent travels included Kosovo and Bogota.

While he was penned in the Barn holding cell, Margos caught sight of Officer Danny Sofer. He made a remark to her, delivered with lip-smacking relish.

```
Surveillance   Transcript:   019-25731   Location   ref:
FARM-0121
------------------------------------------------------------
Danny Sofer (to Margos): Stop staring at my feet, you
Balkan freak!
```

The comment was in an East Armenian dialect, so it was lost on her. However, she remembered the sound of what he'd said, so it could be translated later.

Later, Dutch had it deciphered for her. Margos had said, "Delicious feet!"

Another prisoner being held in the cell said something to Danny along the lines of, "He must like you, the first thing this faggot's said all day." He spoke in a tone that could be described as sneering, disparaging.

Perhaps that was why, soon after, Margos broke the other's neck, killing him.

It's possible that he kills when he thinks he's being disrespected. In this, he's got something in common with many of Farmington's own homegrown thugs.

While being transferred to Central in handcuffs, Margos jimmied open the locked rear door of the detention van and threw himself from it, despite the fact that it was traveling at 40 mph at the time.

He got up and ran away.

Margos is still at large and must be reckoned armed and extremely dangerous.

Rondell Robinson

Rondell started as one of Lionel Phipps's drug-dealing crew. He gave up Phipps to Mackey and became one of his informants. And maybe more.

Rondell grew up in the 'hood with Kern Little, from boyhood days on. It's rumored that hip-hip mogul Little gave his longtime friend Rondell the money that the latter used to establish himself in the drug trade.

Not long before he was killed, Terry Crowley told Aceveda that he'd seen Mackey and Vendrell "conferring" with Robinson. Aceveda believed that Mackey was protecting Rondell's dope business and busting his competitors. It wasn't love, so Mackey must be doing it for money.

But Aceveda had no proof.

Danny Sofer positively identified Rondell as one of the shooters at the Shake Club incident that left four dead. He was arrested and released after posting $100,000 bond.

Rondell's real problem was that he started liking his own product. He was doing too much of what he should have been selling. This further unhinged a personality that wasn't too together to start with. It caused serious lapses in judgment, culminating in his self-destructive feud with Xavier Salaam and Farmington's Nation of Islam mosque.

Rondell Robinson was shot dead, but not by the Muslims. Only someone he'd trusted could have gotten close enough to make the hit. The most likely suspect is his second in command, Tio, who took Rondell's place as the district's favored drug kingpin.

Mrs. Park

Mrs. Park was some of the human flotsam and jetsam thrown up by the hunt for the Streetwalker Strangler. She headed a highly illegal members-only sex club specializing in underage teenage girls. They were largely procured from South Korea, with Mrs. Park arranging to pay the fees to smuggle them into the United States.

In return, they would work off their debt via sex slavery.

At the club, the girls were there to be had. More voyeuristically minded patrons could pay to witness such encounters through a retractable curtain that separated them from the stage.

Mrs. Park was also involved in the making and distribution of so-called Cherrypopper videos, depicting criminally young teen girls losing their virginity on camera. Her partner in this operation was filmmaker Kurt Schmidt.

The hooker called Sally Struthers, the Streetwalker Strangler's fifth victim, had been featured in a Cherrypopper video. The investigation into her murder led to the discovery of Mrs. Park's operation by Vic Mackey, who shut it down.

Hard.

Mrs. Park and Kurt Schmidt are both being held without bail pending trial.

George Michael Klassen

The Gun Club was a licensed gun shop and shooting range. Among its patrons were members of the Latino street gang Toros.

One day, a mass murderer struck at the club. He came in posing as a customer, rented a gun, then strolled along the target range, killing all he found. The target shooters were isolated in their own separate lanes. They wore headphones to muffle the gun reports; so they didn't hear the killer moving from person to person, mowing them down. Before leaving, the killer shot the range owner dead, too.

He slew eight in all. Most were Toros, including the gang leader's pregnant girlfriend.

The killer was revealed to be George Michael Klassen, a racist Anglo who hated Latinos. He struck again, slaying five at a local groceria. One of them was the store owner's son.

The owner managed to come up behind Klassen and knock him out with a baseball bat. He turned Klassen over to the Toros.

Klassen was later shot dead by the boss of the Toros, Train Guttierez.

Train Guttierez

Leader of the Toros.

When Gun Club mass killer George Michael Klassen fell into his hands, Guttierez held him captive while ordering the abduction of Klassen's estranged wife and ten-year-old son. During the abduction, Klassen's in-laws were killed. Guttierez later raped Klassen's wife in front of him and their young son.

```
Surveillance   Transcript:   051-27635   Location   ref:
FARM-1765
------------------------------------------------------------
Guttierez (to Klassen): You didn't see this, huh?
```

Vic Mackey and gang-wise detective Carlos Zamora (from another precinct) tracked Guttierez to his hideout. Guns leveled, they ordered Train to surrender.

For reply, the gang leader shot Klassen dead.

The cops opened fire. Train was wounded but taken alive. Klassen's wife and child were saved.

Hector Estanza

Member of Los Magnificos street gang. Bald, goateed, burly, about 225 pounds. Tattoo of a snake with wings on one arm, a design favored by members of Los Mags. Also had a tattoo of the gang's initials, LM.

A veteran gangbanger with a lengthy, violent criminal record, Estanza was the head of a crew specializing in hijacking trucks—truckjackers. Estanza himself administered brutal beatings to the drivers.

When his girlfriend, Tigre Orozco, tried to tell him they were through, he burned the letter H (for Hector) into her belly. Strike Team member Curtis Lemansky, who was protecting Tigre, gave Estanza a beating in retaliation for the burning.

Estanza and crew were busted by the Strike Team for hijacking a police delivery van transporting items from the Barn's evidence room to Central Storage. The only item taken was a handgun linked to Tigre's brother, Chaco Orozco.

Estanza claimed that it was all a frame-up, that Mackey and company had planted the evidence.

He went to jail.

```
Surveillance  Transcript:  605-42753  Location  ref:
FARM-3877
------------------------------------------------------------
Estanza: You set me up!

Mackey: Yeah, like juries haven't heard that before.
```

Nam Yung

Home invader Nam Yung was a seventeen-year-old Korean American who wanted easy money and knew where to find it. His grandfather, distrustful of banks, kept his life savings hidden away in his house.

Nam Yung and his buddies, Kenny and Paul, gained entrance to his grandfather's house and demanded the money. The elder wouldn't talk, so he and his wife—Nam Yung's grandmother—were tortured to make them tell where the money was hidden.

The grandfather's foot was nailed to the floor to keep him from moving about. Grandmother was shot dead. The money was stolen. When police arrived, the grandfather got hold of a gun and killed himself in front of Julien. He was too ashamed to live.

Detectives Wyms and Wagenbach worked the case. A massive spending spree at a "flash" jewelry store helped lead them to the trio, but not before they had struck again, this time with less lethal consequences. Invading another home, they terrorized the occupants and stole their cash and valuable possessions.

Taken by the police, Nam Yung tried to hang the torture and murder on Kenny and Paul. In justification of his acts, he said, "We just wanted the things what the other kids had."

Pazi Aranbula

Mexican gangster and gunrunner.

With a three-million-peso ($50,000 U.S.) bounty put on him by the Mexican police, Pazi fled north into the United States. He was fingered to the Strike Team by a tipster who said that Pazi was a big cockfight fancier, an aficionado of the fighting game birds. Shane Vendrell went undercover, posing as a redneck gamecock breeder who wanted to trade some fighting birds for illegal guns.

Pazi bit.

Vendrell and Lemansky bagged him. Instead of bringing him in, they traded him to a bounty hunter, in return for half the reward. The bounty hunter returned Pazi to Mexico.

Wally Forton

Wally Forton, white, was dating Melissa Cramer, black. Melissa's mother, Tonya Ann Cramer, strongly disapproved of the relationship and wanted Melissa to end it. Not necessarily because he was white, but because she didn't like him.

Wally went to Tonya Ann Cramer's apartment in the Grove. Also present was Violet Roosevelt, Cramer's sister. An argument broke out. Mrs. Cramer called the police. Forton left the apartment. He waited around outside. No police came.

Twenty minutes later, and still no police, he went back inside. He attacked the women, a long, brutal, drawn-out process, overheard by neighbors, who called 911.

Using a meat tenderizer, Forton bludgeoned both women to death. He then attempted to feed the remains into a kitchen-sink garbage disposal, which quickly clogged up and went dead.

Forton fled the scene. He was long gone by the time the first police unit arrived, almost an hour after the first 911 call had been made.

An hour too late.

Receiving a tip that Forton was in a motel room, the Strike Team and backup units moved on him. They didn't know if Melissa Cramer was alive or dead.

When they broke in with drawn guns, they found her alive, sitting up in bed with Forton. She was unaware of what had happened to her mother and her aunt, unaware of what Forton had done to them.

The police told her.

"Now we can be together," Forton said to her, as he was being led away in handcuffs.

```
Surveillance   Transcript:   039-76532   Location   ref:
FARM-9638
----------------------------------------------------------------
Aceveda: Book him--twice.
```

Twanya, Sonny, and Benji

While she was growing up, Twanya had been raised and helped by Tonya Ann Cramer, one of Wally Forton's victims. She blamed Tonya Ann's death on the cops. If they'd answered the 911 calls in time, like they were supposed to, the victims would still be alive. The cops must pay. It didn't matter which ones, as long as they were cops. She told two male friends, Sonny and Benji, that she wanted to kill cops.

A 911 call was made to the Barn, reporting a disturbance. Two patrol units were dispatched to the locale to investigate. The site was a lonely place.

When the first police car arrived, hidden shooters opened fire on it, killing one officer and seriously wounding the other. A second unit arrived and was also fired on; Officers Sofer and Lowe returned fire, driving the shooters away.

The next day, another bogus 911 call lured a patrol unit into an ambush. This time, two officers were slain and their badges stolen.

A street informant told Mackey that a man had been seen flashing a police badge while boasting of having shot some police.

Sonny was apprehended at the apartment of his father, a heroin addict. The arrest was made by Mackey and Vendrell. A murder gun and police badge were recovered from the suspect.

Sonny said that he'd been tortured by Mackey sticking the pin from a dead officer's badge into his flesh. Claudette Wyms, also present at the scene, said she'd seen no evidence of any such abuse.

Twanya and Benji were hiding out in an abandoned building. It was raided by Aceveda and the Strike Team. Twanya was killed while resisting arrest; Benji was taken alive.

Aceveda parlayed the capture into a media bonanza.

Sedona Tellez

```
Surveillance   Transcript:   022-30457   Location   ref:
FARM-8832
--------------------------------------------------------
Gilroy (to Mackey): She's not just some lay. I love
her.
```

Assistant Chief Ben Gilroy was on his second marriage when Sedona Tellez came to work for him in his office. He fell hard. Once she was sure she had him on a hook, she pitched a moneymaking scheme to him.

Using his police clout, he would destablize an area such as the Grove by diverting police resources to other parts of the district, causing a rise in crime and a drop in real estate values. Operating through front companies chartered in the Cayman Islands, they would buy up the property at depressed rates. Gilroy would then reassign a heavy police presence to the area, cutting crime and causing property values to rise. The properties would then be sold off to developers for a heavy profit.

Some of the money used to buy the properties would be embezzled from police funds, through Tellez's fradulent e-banking.

She had the plan and the expertise; he had the connections. He didn't need much convincing, either.

A hit-and-run accident was their undoing. Dutch Wagenbach found Sedona. Mackey steered Aceveda to the money trail. Aceveda figured out the scheme, then got Sedona to roll on Gilroy.

```
Surveillance  Transcript:  044-33376  Location  ref:
FARM-1308
-------------------------------------------------------------
Aceveda: Vic, this is Sedona Tellez. . . . She has a
lot of interesting things to say about our assistant
chief.


Mackey: So much for loyalty, huh, lady?


Sedona: Ben's in love. I have a future.
```

Ben Gilroy

Surveillance Transcript: 038-76798 Location ref:
FARM-8731

Gilroy: We're dinosaurs, Vic, and make no mistake--
the meteor's coming.

Even after being busted, Gilroy wouldn't go away. He returned once more to plague Vic Mackey, showing up drunk at the Mackey house. Mackey hustled him away. Gilroy was supposed to be under house arrest, but he'd gotten rid of his electronic ankle bracelet monitor and gone on the run.

Sedona Tellez had raided their bank accounts, taken the money, and disappeared, Gilroy said. He still had about $70,000 stashed away. He said he couldn't do prison time and begged Mackey to help him get out of the country.

Surveillance Transcript: 011-12876 Location ref:
FARM-7693

Gilroy: I got greedy. I lost everything. There's a
lesson there, Vic.

Later that day, Mackey went to see Aceveda. Lanie Kellis was there, too. Mackey said that Gilroy had come to him and that he'd left him drunk in his apartment. He was reporting him because Gilroy was a fugitive.

Aceveda asked why Mackey hadn't brought Gilroy in. Mackey said that he wanted Gilroy to sober up first. Aceveda sent a patrol unit out to pick up Gilroy, but when they arrived at the apartment, he was gone.

Kellis was upset. It turned out she'd known about Gilroy's run, that she'd had some police department headquarters detectives watching him. Working with the district attorney, she'd arranged for Gilroy's release so he could get proof about the charges he'd raised against Vic Mackey.

Somehow Gilroy had backdoored his shadows and given them the slip, losing them. He's still at large, whereabouts unknown. It is believed he might be in Mexico, but this is only guesswork.

Armando "Armadillo" Quintero

From Sinaloa, Mexico. Tested high I.Q.; at age eleven he was put in a school for the gifted. Shortly after, he raped a teacher and was sentenced to two years in juvenile prison. After that, he was smart enough to keep his record clean.

While his brother, Navaro, was taking care of business in Mexico, Armadillo began making moves in Farmington, seeking to unite all the Latino street gangs into one supergang. He raped twelve-year-old Mayda, and burned competing drug dealers to death.

After the murder of Tio, Armadillo's face was badly burned from being held down against a hot stovetop coil. The most likely suspect in the burning was Mackey.

Armadillo's next move was to flood the schools with heroin. When Mackey tried to restrain him by threatening to greenlight the imprisoned Navaro and have him killed, Armadillo saved him the trouble.

He himself greenlit his brother, who was knifed to death in prison. Armadillo beat and tortured Strike Team member Ronnie Gardocki, burning his face to send Mackey a message.

While in the Barn holding cell, Armadillo was stabbed to death by another prisoner. He took his secrets to the grave.

```
Surveillance   Transcript:   035-15772   Location   ref:
FARM-1323
-----------------------------------------------------------
Armadillo (to Wyms): Every scar is a victory.
```

Navaro Quintero

Junior of the Quintero brothers. Wanted in the United States on multiple federal drug and racketeering counts, Navaro Quintero fled to Tijuana, Mexico. He took care of the drug business at that end.

A major trafficker, he supplied crooked Customs Officer Jasper with poison-laced cocaine to destabilize Farmington district drug dealers competing against Armadillo.

Navaro was apprehended by the Strike Team and handed over to federal authorities. He charged Mackey's squad had abducted him in Mexico, extorted a $400,000 ransom, and then double-crossed him by keeping the money and not freeing him.

Farmington File Photo: Case #72-X. Subject: Navaro Quintero bust.

Armadillo didn't arrange to kill his brother—honest.

143

They then illegally transported him into the United States, drugged and in a car trunk.

Navaro's claims were found baseless by U.S. authorities.

While in prison, he was shanked—stabbed to death by another inmate. Did Navaro die thinking that Mackey had greenlit him?

Or did he know that it was his own brother, Armadillo, who'd had him hit?

Fleetwood Walker

Fleetwood was a dealer in stolen goods. When Mackey's old partner Joe Clarke lost his temper and knocked Fleetwood's teeth out in public, in front of witnesses, he lost his job and Fleetwood won a $1.2 million award as settlement for the police brutality suit he'd filed against the city.

Even though he was a rich man, Fleetwood couldn't stay out of the game. He continued fencing stolen goods, such as warehouse electronics, with a sideline in automatic weapons.

Mackey and Clarke got a lead on him and moved in. In the shootout that followed, one of Fleetwood's crew shot Mackey, wounding him. Mackey killed his shooter.

Fleetwood managed to escape, but was later tracked down and caught by Clarke and the other Strike Team members.

He should have quit when he was ahead.

Mike Holden

Holden was a firefighter with a penchant for wife beating and three-way sex with hookers (though not at the same time). His wife finally walked out on him, taking their two kids with her. She sought refuge in a battered women's shelter. Its location was confidential, but Holden had a friend on the force who gave him the address.

Holden first sent a hooker "friend" of his into the shelter as his spy, to make sure that his wife was inside.

She was.

Holden went in and killed every adult woman on the premises—six in all, including his wife. The children there he left alone, except for his four-year-old son, whom he took with him. His two-year-old daughter he left behind.

He holed up in a sleazy motel, keeping himself supplied with a steady flow of hookers. He'd have one hooker babysit his son while he had sex with another. Then the hookers would switch, with him having sex with the babysitter while the other one looked after the kid.

Mackey's hooker CI Connie Riesler found Holden and got inside the motel room. She tipped Mackey to the location, but things went sour. Holden killed Connie and was cut down by police snipers.

Jackson and Carlson

Paul Jackson and Ray Carlson were uniformed Barn cops. Jackson is believed to have been the ringleader in the alleged blanket party thrown by him, Carlson, and Julien Lowe to give a beating to Frank, the HIV-positive prisoner who'd bitten Danny Sofer.

When Julien was outed for being gay, it was his turn to get the treatment from the other two cops.

Jackson and Carlson instituted a vicious campaign of abuse against him. Scurrilous posters with his picture were pinned up on the bulletin board. An anonymous telephone caller said obscene things about Julien to his ten-year-old stepson, Randall. After that, Julien and Jackson clashed physically, fighting in the station in front of the prisoners in the holding cell.

Danny Sofer reported the pattern of harassment to Captain Aceveda, who saw to it that Jackson and Carlson were fired with cause.

Shortly after, several as yet unidentified persons gave Julien Lowe a blanket party, savagely beating him with nightsticks. Jackson and Carlson must be ranked as prime suspects in that investigation.

Malcolm Rama

Why did Malcolm Rama bludgeon an elderly man nearly to death?

Dutch Wagenbach had the case. Catching the suspect was easy—Malcolm had stepped in a pool of the victim's blood and literally left a trail almost to his front door. But Dutch wanted to know why.

He knew that juries liked to know why, too. Juries like motives.

Malcolm Rama was a teenager of Thai extraction. Back in Thailand, in the northern hill country, the Rama clan and the Kusa clan have fought an eight-hundred-year-old blood feud, marked by rape, murder, and massacre. That meant nothing to Malcolm Rama, or so he thought.

Then he met Li Kusa, 60.

A Kusa! Malcolm thought it was funny. He told his father, but his father wasn't laughing. He flew into a rage, threatening to kill Li Kusa, a man he'd never met. Malcolm was able to calm his father only by saying he'd do something about it.

He worked as a volunteer at a Thai cultural center. He stole a Thai relic, a war club, and took it with him when he went to confront Li Kusa. When he identified himself as a Rama, the other spat in his face.

Malcolm hammered the old man with the club, beating him nearly to death.

Once caught, Malcolm Rama himself was bewildered about how he'd come to be where he was, a prisoner in jail charged with attempted murder.

The only explanation he could come up with was that he'd somehow gotten caught up in the ages-long feud, that it felt right, that he'd found some kind of identity by acting on behalf of his ancient clan.

```
Surveillance   Transcript:   039-96854   Location   ref:
FARM-1366
-----------------------------------------------------------
Dutch: Until you know why, a detective's job isn't
done.
```

IAD Surveillance Photo: #31.
Subject: Offcrs. Sofer and Lowe
canvassing the neighborhood.

Stanley the Aerosol Guy

People bugged Stanley.

Like the regular at the local lunch counter. Every day, during a busy lunch hour, one customer on line could never make up his mind what to order. All there was to order was hot dogs and hamburgers and he knew that, but he kept on stalling.

One day, while this customer was doing his time-wasting thing, Stanley pulled out an aerosol spray can and said, "You're bugging me."

Then he sprayed the time-waster in the eyes with bug spray, temporarily blinding him.

Encouraged by Dutch, who was mentoring her detective work, Danny Sofer did some sleuthing of her own, tracking down the aerosol assailant by canvassing the neighborhood stores for information on any recent purchasers of bug spray.

It paid off. She found Stanley and arrested him, handcuffing him. When he tried to rationalize his crimes as petty mischief, she told him that he would be charged with assault with a deadly weapon.

Stanley said, "Now you're starting to bug me."

Dante Fell

Dante Fell was an OG (Original Gangster), a veteran Farmington banger and a leader and founder of the black street gang the Compton Crowns. A successful gangster, he'd since graduated to national affairs, handling the chores of organizing new CC branches in other U.S. cities.

While doing so, he'd racked up numerous federal warrants for assault, armed robbery, racketeering, drug trafficking, murder, and many more. He was a fugitive wanted by the feds, who'd been unable to catch him.

Word hit the street that Fell had returned to the Farm. It came at the same time that the Kellis report hit the newspapers, wrapping the precinct in bad press. The Barn badly needed a win.

Mackey knew that hip-hop music producer Kern Little was an old friend of Fell's. He made Little a lot of promises to get him to give up a lead toward finding the fugitive.

The Strike Team and plenty of backup units moved in on Mission Cross Hospital, where Fell had gone to visit his girlfriend, who'd just given birth to their first child, a boy. After being allowed to hold his infant son for a moment, Fell surrendered peacefully.

Jeffrey Cole

Fourteen-year-old son of a mixed marriage (black father, white mother). His parents were divorced; he lived with his mother. Jeffrey Cole was reported to

the precinct as a missing person. Fueling fears for his safety was the fact that he'd been seen on a street corner where male hustlers hawked their wares. Jeffrey Cole was last spotted getting into a car driven by an older man.

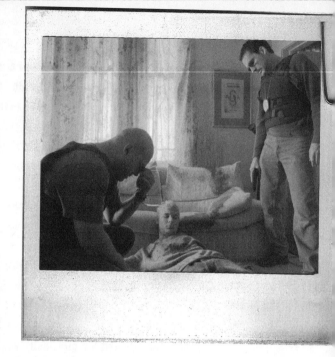

Soon after, a youth of around the same age, Lydell Crouch, also went missing. Now came the fear that both boys had fallen victim to a serial killer who'd struck before in the area. His signature was to separately abduct two young teen boys. He would sexually assault and torture his victims, then shoot them in their faces and dump the bodies weeks apart.

Dutch Wagenbach was working on the assumption that Lydell Crouch and Jeffrey Cole were captives of the killer. It turned out that Lydell Crouch's killer was none other than Jeffrey Cole. They went to the same school. Crouch was black, while Cole buddied up with white supremacists (who were unaware that Cole's father was black).

Cole and Crouch had quarreled. Cole had been working the hustler's corner so he could find a gay john to mug. He needed money to buy a gun; then he used the gun to kill Crouch.

When police closed in on him, Jeffrey Cole refused to drop his weapon and surrender. He was shot dead by Curtis Lemansky. A search revealed that Cole had made a death list of other teens he hated and was planning to massacre them Columbine-style.

The "double-feature" serial killer remains unknown and uncaught.

Lops

Lops is short for lopsided, which describes the shape of his head. Lops was a leader of the Johnnies, a black street gang that had been eclipsed by the Latino gangs but was looking to make a comeback in the power vacuum left by the death of Armadillo.

To cement his power and bring on the fear, Lops revived an old Johnnies custom: killing a civilian on April Fools' Day for every gang member who'd been slain in the previous year. This year, three members of the Johnnies had died, so three citizens must be cut down at random by gang executioners.

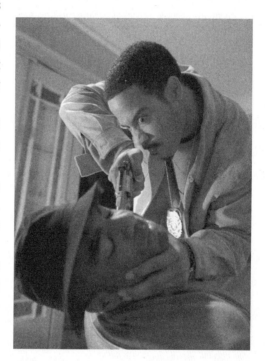

The first victim was Jeff Franklin, Claudette Wyms's ex-husband.

Mackey and Tavon Garris were the first to get to Lops. With a gun to his head, Lops talked, naming the shooters.

Mackey and Garris took down the third and last shooter at a street fair, before he killed anybody.

Alex Eznik

Shane Vendrell's stolen badge turned up on the black market, where it was bought by Hrach, a member of Alex Eznik's Armenian crime mob. A clerk at a hot ice chop shop—a jewelry store where stolen diamonds are recut and resold—was also a member of the same mob.

Flashing the badge and posing as a cop, Hrach gained entrance to the store, where he killed the clerk and stole a bag of jewels.

A tipster named Tike put Mackey and Vendrell on to Hrach, in exchange for a third of the recovered diamonds. The detectives bagged Hrach, penning him in the Barn. Hrach gave them an opportunity to get their foot in the door of Alex Eznik's operation.

Mackey needed Aceveda's authorization. He said that he and Vendrell would pose as crooked cops to bait Eznik.

Crooked cops! Aceveda got a laugh out of that one. He gave the okay.

After contacting Eznik and going to his club, Mackey and Vendrell gave him two-thirds of the diamonds Hrach had stolen. Eznik didn't like that the other third was missing, but Mackey said that was the way it had to be.

To further Eznik's interest, Mackey tipped him off about an imminent raid of one of his hot-car garages.

Eznik expressed interest in having Hrach killed in jail. Mackey countered by offering to deliver Hrach to him.

The next phase of the sting required a freshly dead man—of which there was no shortage on the Farm. All they had to do was wait for a while and one would turn up.

One did, a man who'd committed suicide by gunshot. Mackey and Vendrell dressed him in Hrach's clothes, then obliterated his face with a shotgun. Eznik bought into the idea that it was Hrach.

Mackey set up a deal where he would access confidential law enforcement

computer files to learn which of Eznik's operations were objects of police interest or surveillance. To do this, he must know the locations.

Eznik asked to have his man Hagop accompany Mackey to the Barn. He would name the locations and Mackey would check them off against the computer to see if they were listed or not.

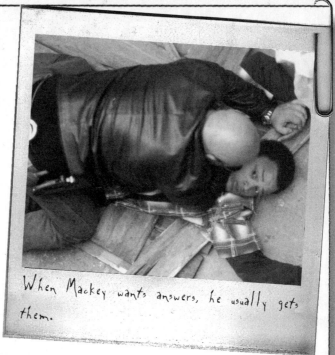

When Mackey wants answers, he usually gets them.

The two went to the station, while Vendrell stayed behind with Eznik as insurance. The plan soured when Eznik's man inadvertently caught sight of Hrach alive and well at the precinct house.

Strike Team and backup units swooped into Eznik's headquarters, busting him and his mob and rescuing Vendrell.

Before Hrach's untimely appearance soured the plan, Mackey had still managed to collect a nice list of Eznik's crime-related properties, all of which were raided and busted. All except one.

The only one not a crime site was a warehouse at 9210 Escovida. Rumors have surfaced that the site was the locale for the so-called Money Train, "a rolling bank vault," an operation that laundered the Armenian mob's West Coast take—a potential multimillion-dollar score.

The money-drop site would surely have been shut down by the mob as soon as it learned of the Eznik arrest.

When the warehouse at 9210 Escovida was investigated, it was found to be only . . . an empty warehouse.

In this district, if they're not actually shooting at you, they qualify for this category.

Detective Tom Gannon (Retired)

A veteran detective, Gannon was legendary for cracking the Beechwood Canyon Slasher case, where he tagged the stepbrother as the killer who'd massacred most of the rest of his family. He was nearing the sunset of his career when he was assigned to the Barn at its start-up.

Dutch Wagenbach was impressed by the great sleuth, but the feeling wasn't mutual. Gannon took Dutch for something of a horse's ass and tagged him as the precinct "rube"—the butt, a figure of fun, a joke.

He stopped laughing during the hunt for a ring of Mexican kidnappers who preyed on Salvadoran immigrants. He concentrated on a witness he believed could identify them. Claudette Wyms disagreed, thinking that ransom broker Latigo could be persuaded to help catch the kidnappers.

Gannon didn't think much of that approach and went his own way.

Wagenbach thought otherwise, teaming with Wyms to follow up her angle. Latigo cooperated and the kidnappers were caught.

That success led to the professional pairing of Claudette and Dutch.

Gannon was on his way to retirement when he started at the Barn. He never adjusted to it. One of the cases he was working on at the time of his retirement was the unsolved murder of real estate broker Kyle Kelner.

Dutch wound up working the case (with Shane Vendrell!), and he met the deceased's widow, Kim. He solved the case and caught the killer.

He also solved the mystery of what to do on Saturday nights, by entering into a relationship with Kim Kelner.

Connie Riesler

Life on the street is hard. Few know that better than the street hookers, curb-side prostitutes who troll for cruising johns and turn tricks with them in their cars. Theirs is a sordid existence of brutalization, degradation, arrests, and alcohol and drug abuse. What youth and beauty they have gets used up fast; then they're pushed aside by newer, fresher recruits.

Such a one was Connie. Finding herself six months pregnant, she tried to induce an abortion via the use of powdered drain cleaner and a plumber's rubber plunger. Vic Mackey found her in a cheap hotel, on the bathroom floor, lying in a pool of blood. She was rushed to the hospital, where she delivered a baby boy ten weeks premature. His name was Brian.

Mackey took notice. Brian was a tough kid. That got his respect.

Brian got well enough for Connie to take him home. She had her mother take care of the baby while she was out on the streets, tricking. At the time the Barn opened, Connie was part of a stable of hookers run by Ringo the pimp. Another hooker in that same stable was Rhonda, victim of a drive-by shooting ordered by Lionel Phipps in his bid to expand into the "protection" racket, squeezing the local pimps and hookers.

It's known that Connie was in contact with Mackey at this time.

Connie went to see Phipps at his place, to bend the knee and bow down to his street thug's authority. He gave her a beating, just on "general principles."

Soon after, Rondell Robinson signed a statement saying that he'd recently dropped off a load of crack cocaine at Phipps's place. That allowed Aceveda to get out a search warrant, which was served by Mackey's Strike Team and backup units.

A cache of crack coke was found hidden in the bathroom. Phipps denied ownership, claiming it had been planted.

If the drugs were planted, Connie would make a likely suspect. Rhonda was her friend, giving her a motive for wanting revenge on Phipps. And she was Mackey's informant.

Phipps's high-profile bust was a feather in Mackey's cap, buying him the time to get the Strike Team up and running the way he wanted without interference from higher-ups.

In any case, Phipps went to prison for the shooting, the drive-by guns also being found in his place.

But they wouldn't have been found without the search warrant for the crack cocaine.

Connie also supplied the tip that led to the raid on drug dealer Two-Time, resulting in his death and that of Detective Terry Crowley.

While out food shopping, Connie's mother suffered a fatal stroke. Connie and Brian's safety net was gone. Who would look after Brian while Connie was out working?

She couldn't afford to hire a nursemaid or sitter. She didn't dare apply for help at one of the welfare agencies, for fear that they'd find out about her drug habit and take Brian away from her and place him in a foster home.

She decided to "get straight," to go cold turkey to overcome her addiction. While doubtful, Mackey pitched in and helped out. He had his wife, Corrine, take care of Brian while Connie was kicking.

It was a tough sell. He had to do some fast talking to convince Corrine that the baby wasn't his.

```
Surveillance  Transcript:  012-62273  Location  ref:
FARM-2664
-----------------------------------------------------------
Connie: Vic and me have a bond that transcends sex.
```

Connie was his informant. She'd helped him out in the past and now he'd do the same for her. The plight of mother and child had gotten under even his crocodile-thick skin.

Across town, Connie was in a hotel room, detoxing. Ronnie Gardocki was babysitting her.

It was rough. She withstood her own private hell of kicking for as many hours as she could, but it was too much.

While Ronnie was out of the room getting her a glass of water, she clipped some money from his wallet, sneaked outside, and copped some dope.

The noble experiment had failed. Connie went back on the streets. Baby Brian was given up for adoption.

Connie spent ninety days in jail and came out clean. She wanted to go to work for Mackey as a Confidential Informant (CI). She'd already worked as his informant but this was different. A CI was registered with the department and had to sign a contract agreeing to provide four solid tips per month. The CI is paid $2,000 per month.

She had a dream of using the CI gig to get her life together and reclaim Brian. Mackey quietly and seriously told her the facts of life: Brian was out of her life and she wasn't going to get him back.

He agreed to try her out as a CI. Connie tipped him to Felipe Gomez, a drug dealer who was moving heroin to schoolkids. By following the lead, Mackey was able to stop Armadillo Quintero's heroin blitz of the schools, and ultimately find Quintero himself.

But that came later.

A $5,000 reward was posted for information leading to the arrest of the Battered Women's Shelter Slayer, fireman Mike Holden.

Connie wanted that reward—she was still clinging to the dream of getting Brian back.

Holden liked hookers and had a steady supply of them parading in and out of the sleazy motel where he was hiding out with his four-year-old son.

Using her street connections, Connie got inside the motel room and found Holden. She contacted Mackey, but was trapped inside the room with another hooker, Holden's kid, and Holden.

Holden was already suspicious of Connie. When he heard police sirens approach, he pulled a gun and held them hostage. Mackey came in unarmed, offering himself as a hostage.

Holden's killing rage flared up and he shot Connie. Mackey tore down the window curtains, exposing Holden to deadly sniper fire.

Connie was dead. The department refused to pay for her funeral, so Mackey paid for it himself.

Van Bro

A one-eyed, wheelchair-bound black man, Van Bro is a painter who sells his canvases from a sidewalk stand. He's also a tipster who trades information for Vic Mackey's money. Every now and then, someone on the Strike Team has to keep Van Bro happy by buying a painting.

```
Surveillance  Transcript:  015-72983  Location  ref:
FARM-1072
---------------------------------------------------------------
Van Bro: Don't be hangin' it in no bathroom.
```

Van Bro helped in the hunt for the 911 shooters. When Armadillo Quintero put out hits on the Strike Team, he furnished a hot lead to the whereabouts of Quazi, an underling who helped point the way to Armadillo's capture.

Some thugs worked him over and stole his wheelchair.

The Strike Team bought him a new one.

Jorge Machado

A political powerhouse in the L.A. Latino community and beyond, Machado was the guiding force behind the construction of the Project Familia housing development. He can deliver large numbers of voters to the polls on election day. He's wired into dozens of funds, foundations, government projects, do-good businesses, antigang activities.

David Aceveda approached Machado, asking for his backing for a run for the district's city council seat.

Machado agreed, liking Aceveda's appeal to the rising Latino demographic and his universal appeal as a reform-minded cop who was not afraid to go against the department in the interests of justice. He served as Aceveda's campaign manager.

By the time the polls closed on primary day, Aceveda had won. He was halfway to a seat on the city council.

Now all he has to do is beat his opponent in the fall on election day.

He will, if Jorge Machado has anything to say about it.

And he does.

Chaco Orozco

Former Los Mags banger; after jail time served and released on parole, Chaco decided to leave the Life. He was a two-time loser; under California's Three Strikes Law, with two previous offenses on his record, conviction on a third could send him to prison for life.

He joined the antigang program Clean Slate, attended meetings regularly, and began the painful process of having his gang tattoos lasered off his skin. He looked like he was turning his life around.

So it was a setback, to say the least, when he was shot by Strike Team detective Curtis Lemansky.

Mackey and Lemansky had gone to the house of Tigre Orozco, Chaco's sister. They were looking for Hector Estanza, head of a crew of Los Mags truckjackers. Estanza was Tigre's boyfriend.

When Chaco saw Mackey and Lemansky, he ran. He looked like he was reaching for a weapon, so Lemansky shot him. A gun that allegedly belonged to Chaco was found at the scene. Chaco went to the hospital.

Digging around, Mackey and Lemansky had to change their estimation of Chaco. Tigre was on the outs with Estanza, and Chaco had been at the house to protect her. Now Lemansky guarded her. Sparks must have been struck, because according to reports filed by Tigre's parole officer, she's in a relationship with Lemansky.

Hector Estanza was arrested for hijacking a police delivery van and stealing Chaco's gun, which was never seen again. Without the gun, all charges against Chaco were dropped.

Of course, the fact remains that Lemansky shot Chaco, putting him in the hospital.

Kern Little

Farmington's own, Little is an ambitious man who's risen far. As a hip-hop music producer, he has generated many hits and is much in demand by artists of that genre. Professing a desire to "keep it real," he placed his recording studio in the Farm.

It is believed that the money that Little used to establish himself as a legitimate music businessman came from drug dealing. In this context, please note Little's longtime association with

IAD Surveillance Photo: #62A.
Subject: Kern Little.

Rondell Robinson, whom he's known since boyhood days.

More than one source has claimed that Little gave Robinson big money to establish himself in the drug trade. Robinson and two of his posse were identified as the shooters in the Shake Club killings.

After that, the relationship became strained. Little held Rondell responsible for getting hip-hop music artist Tyesha so high on drugs that she'd been unable to perform at a recording session, running up costly studio expenses.

Soon after that, Rondell was found shot dead.

The relationship between Little and Vic Mackey became strained over the Dante Fell case. Little needed money. His recording studio was spending cash faster than he could make it. He missed his cut of the loot, which had been regularly passed to him by the dealers when he'd been in on the trade.

Mackey agreed to the deal. He got Fell, but Little got screwed. Mackey said he wasn't going to deliver on a partnership reestablishing Little's drug empire. There was no deal. He admitted he'd lied to Little, played him to get Fell.

For Kern Little, Vic Mackey is a man who doesn't do what he says he'll do. How far he wants to push it, though, remains to be seen.

Xavier Salaam

Born Xavier Criss, Salaam served six years of a ten-year term at Chino State Prison for manslaughter. While inside, he experienced a religious conversion to Islam, in the form of the doctrines followed by the Nation of Islam. After his release, he eventually established himself as the leader of the group's mosque in Farmington.

Some of the mosque's street preachers ran afoul of Rondell Robinson, whose drug dealers also wanted to occupy the same corner. The Muslims were beaten by thugs.

Soon after, while Rondell was sitting in a parked car with Kern Little, he was attacked in a drive-by shooting. His and Little's lives were spared because the car was armored and equipped with bulletproof glass—useful options for hip-hop music producers in the Farmington 'hood.

Rondell thought the Muslims were behind the shooting. He ordered a drive-by in retaliation, and some of them were wounded.

This prompted mosque leader Xavier Salaam to lead a dozen of his men on a march to the Barn, where they stationed themselves in an outer lobby, refusing to leave until police took decisive action against Robinson.

Salaam stated to Captain Aceveda his belief that Robinson had thrived due in large part to his having police protection. Challenged by Aceveda to name the source of that "protection," Salaam said that he'd rather wait until he had more solid proof.

Salaam's action was classic nonviolent civil disobedience. He and his members blocked no access, interfered with no comings and goings, initiated no violent moves. But they would not go. They simply would not leave.

When Rondell Robinson's body was found shot dead, they left.

```
Surveillance  Transcript:  059-32378  Location  ref:
FARM-3611
-----------------------------------------------------------
Xavier Salaam: We will not rest until the dealers and
the police who give them comfort are brought to justice.
```

Tio

Born Theodore Osmond, Tio began as drug trafficker Rondell Robinson's lieutenant. The ambitious underling watched coolly as Rondell began overusing his own product, leading to such lapses in judgment as clashing with the mosque's street preachers.
That persuaded him that Rondell must go. It wouldn't hurt for Kern Little to go

with him, either. It wasn't Xavier Salaam but rather Tio who ordered a drive-by on Rondell—and Little. The attempt failed, but Rondell never suspected it was his own subordinate who'd tried to have him hit.

A follow-up attempt was more successful, resulting in Robinson's execution-style murder. His place was filled by Tio, the chief beneficiary of Rondell's murder.

Farmington File Photo: 911 Killer Case #396-A. Subject: Tio Osmond Interrogation.

During the hunt for the 911 ambush killers, Tio (through his people on the street) got good information, helping to catch one of the killers.

```
Surveillance  Transcript:  018-48011  Location  ref:
FARM-1532
-----------------------------------------------------------
Tio: A lot of people say the cops had it coming. I
say we've got to work with the police.
```

Tio's reign as drug kingpin was short-lived, however. As was he. His operation crumbled under the ferocious onslaught of Armadillo Quintero.

First, one of his buildings was torched.

Next, several of his crew were torched.

Then he was torched, necklaced with a gasoline-doused tire hung over his shoulders and set ablaze, burning him alive.

Ms. Emerich

Administrator at Glen Ridge, a special-needs school for autistic children.

With their son, Matthew, having been diagnosed as autistic, Vic and Corrine Mackey sought to take him out of public school, where he was fast falling behind, and place him in the more nurturing environment of a private school solely for autistic children.

Glen Ridge is such a place.

Mackey was ready to pay the $25,000-a-year tuition. Matthew was initially accepted to the school, only to be put on a waiting list and later rejected. The rejection coincided with the bad press about the alleged Farmington cop drug thefts, some of which named Mackey as a suspect.

Mackey learned that, a few months earlier, Ms. Emerich had reported a home burglary. A number of valuables had been stolen, including a ring that was a family heirloom.

Mackey got on the case. Using his contacts with tipsters and fences of stolen property, he soon recovered the ring and returned it to Ms. Emerich.

Subsequently, it was discovered that a mistake had been made and that Matthew Mackey would be enrolled for the coming term at Glen Ridge.

Karen Mitchell

Karen Mitchell was an assistant to City Councilman Morgan. She was also Morgan's handpicked candidate for the Sixth District's council seat. That put her and David Aceveda in competition for the party nomination. A primary would decide who would be the victor and go on to represent the party on election day in the fall.

When 911 delays led to the brutal murders of two women, sparking community unrest, Karen Mitchell raced to the scene, appearing as Morgan's representative. It was a touchy political situation: she was monitoring the performance of Aceveda, her rival in the upcoming primary.

The 911 tapes, containing the repeated calls for help from Tonya Ann Cramer and Violet Roosevelt as they tried to fend off their attacker, were grisly stuff. Horrific. Damning.

Somebody leaked them to the press. It wasn't Aceveda. There was nothing in it for him to surface those inflammatory tapes.

Karen Mitchell had access to the tapes, and certainly had the motive. However, there's no proof that she was the leaker.

Catching the 911 ambush killers and Assistant Chief Gilroy gave Aceveda a fifteen-point lead in the polls. Armadillo's heroin epidemic in the schools knocked it down. Mitchell was quick to capitalize on the problem, appearing at one of the affected schools and holding a press conference on the steps, denouncing police (i.e., Aceveda's) ineptitude.

The leaking of the Kellis report critical of the precinct came right before election day. The *Times* endorsed Mitchell over Aceveda, giving her another boost.

Going into primary day, Karen Mitchell was four points up. When the polls finally closed, she was down.

The winner: Aceveda.

Lanie Kellis

In the wake of the riots and the Gilroy mess, the city council sent Lanie Kellis, a civilian auditor, to monitor the Barn. Her real purpose, though, was to get something on Aceveda. He had enemies on the council. They hadn't liked his making lemonade out of lemons and coming out of the Two Days of Blood with a hefty lead in the polls.

Kellis was no mere figurehead. As civilian auditor, she had real power: the power to institute changes, to recommend hirings and firings, and to pass judgment on whether the Farmington precinct experiment was a failure or a success.

Neither Mackey nor Aceveda needed her looking over their shoulders. Aceveda had an election to win and Mackey had to deal with Armadillo and all the other irons he had in the fire.

Kellis was initially impressed with Mackey, recommending him for a Medal of Valor for his actions in busting Fleetwood's gunrunning operation. Later, though, she turned against him.

This explains Ben Gilroy's postarrest appeal to Vic Mackey. Gilroy was working with Kellis and the district attorney. He was offered a deal if he could get something on Mackey, something that would hold up in court. They were especially interested in Mackey's role in the death of Terry Crowley.

Gilroy was equipped with a miniature tape recorder. From the time he left the D.A.'s office, he was tailed by detectives.

He was taken to an apartment by Mackey and Shane Vendrell. Soon after, Mackey and Vendrell left. The detectives remained in place outside the building, watching for Gilroy.

They didn't watch hard enough. Somehow Gilroy gave them the slip, eluding them by going out a side exit.

He has not been seen since.

The tape recorder was left behind. In it was a tape of Mackey and Gilroy talking. They said nothing incriminating.

In fact, the conversation was so innocuous that a cynic might have thought it was a setup.

Kellis's long-awaited final report on the Barn was two weeks short of being finished when someone leaked it. (It would be nice to know who that someone was. So far, not a clue.)

Inevitably, the Kellis report surfaced in the press, putting the blame for the precinct's problems on the Aceveda-Mackey alliance. She had nothing solid enough to hang them with, just enough to tar them with.

They could take it. They'd both been on the receiving end of worse: Aceveda with the Maureen Wilmore rape story, Mackey with the alleged drug theft.

Kellis also found that the precinct generally served a useful purpose and recommended that it continue to remain in operation.

The negative publicity generated by the report—which hit the headlines a day or two before primary election day—was offset by the positive press generated by Julien Lowe's heroic apprehension of a carjacker and rescue of the infant in the stolen car, and by the Strike Team's apprehension of Compton Crowns gang chief Dante Fell, wanted on numerous federal charges for racketeering, drug dealing, extortion, murder, etc.

The main weakness of the Kellis report, however, was its failure to get the hard facts needed to take before a grand jury to get some indictments. She named Mackey's Strike Team as the epicenter of the trouble at the Barn, but had no hard evidence to back up the charges.

Gordie Liman

Topflight private investigators don't come cheap. But with Gordie Liman, you get results. Not always the ones you want.

After the Gilroy scare, Corrine Mackey left Vic, taking the kids with her. She didn't say where she was going.

Mackey hired Gordie Liman to find them. Like most private eyes, Gordie's an ex-cop. He tracked them to Colorado Springs, then to Phoenix, then back to California. He told Mackey he'd traced Corrine to a motel, where she was staying with a boyfriend. Mackey broke into the room, gun in hand.

It wasn't Corrine. The couple in bed were shocked and scared. Mackey mumbled an apology and got out of there, fast.

Gordie said he was sorry, real sorry. Still, Mackey was a cop himself. He knew these things happened.

After Mackey was shot, Corrine and the kids returned. Later, when Armadillo put out hits on the Strike Team, Mackey paid Gordie and his operatives to watch his kids at school, going to and coming from, and during recess.

The danger passed. Gordie told Mackey that Corrine had been to see a divorce lawyer a couple of times. He urged Mackey to get some legal protection. He put him together with a high-powered divorce attorney, who had Vic file divorce papers against Corrine as a protective measure.

It turned out that Gordie was half right. Corrine had been to see the divorce lawyer, at the urging of her friends mostly. She decided not to go through with it and saw him one last time to sign some papers to get some of her retainer back.

She was stunned when Vic served her with divorce papers—so shocked she had to rush over to his apartment to confront him. Where she found him with another woman.

Gordie Liman, himself, is divorced.

Tulips

Tulips and Shane Vendrell met in the line of things. She was a dancer at a strip club; he was working undercover. A bait-and-bash racket was being run out of the club. Dancers would get patrons, usually drunks, excited, then offer to go outside with them and "finish them off."

Outside, while the mark was distracted, a male accomplice would assault him with a tire iron, knocking him out and robbing him.

It was only a matter of time before someone got killed.

The Strike Team was on stakeout outside the club. Vendrell had gone in wearing a wire. The others could hear him on the receiver in the parked van where they waited. He emerged with Tulips, who really had him going pretty good.

A man rushed up out of the alley and clubbed him with a tire iron.

Hearing the whole thing, the other squad members rushed up and busted Tulips and her accomplice. His name was Carl and he was Tulips's "boyfriend."

At the Barn, they were held in separate rooms so they couldn't cook up a story together. Tulips claimed that the racket was Carl's idea and that he'd forced her into cooperating. Carl said that it was her idea and that she'd dragged him into it.

Vendrell was alone with Tulips in an interrogation room. They had sex. Vendrell was so besotted that he hadn't even thought to first switch off the video camera monitoring the room.

Anybody watching the screen would have gotten quite a show.

While Vendrell was having sex with a female prisoner, Lemansky was collecting information from the other dancers indicating that Tulips was the originator of the scheme.

Tulips threatened to report Vendrell to the higher-ups if she wasn't allowed to walk on the charges. She had a fresh load of Vendrell's DNA to prove that they'd had sex.

With Vendrell compromised, the squad was forced to release Tulips, while laying the heavy charges on the boyfriend.

Vendrell was steamed. He knew he'd been played. He called Tulips a "penis flytrap."

Months later, she walked back into his life, seeking him out at the Barn. She wanted something, of course. She was mad at an ex-boyfriend and wanted him busted. He was a drug dealer and she was willing to set him up.

Vendrell was reluctant but it was an easy bust and Mackey wanted it.

Vendrell posed as Tulips's new boyfriend, also a drug dealer. He sold the ex a bagful of Viagra, then busted him.

Back at the Barn, Tulips showed her appreciation to Vendrell by doing him in the interrogation room.

Just like old times—but this time he covered the camera.

Joe Clarke

Veteran crime-busting African-American police officer who was Vic Mackey's old partner in the pre-Barn days.

A good (if excessively rough) cop, Clarke met his Waterloo courtesy of Fleetwood, a fence whose teeth he'd knocked out. He made the mistake of doing it in front of witnesses. The city paid Fleetwood $1.2 million to make his lawsuit go away.

It made Joe Clarke's career in law enforcement go away, too. He was kicked off the force. His pension and set-aside money were eaten up by legal fees, impoverishing him. He lost his family, after his wife took the kids and left him.

In Joe Clarke, Mackey might well be seeing a preview of his own bleak future.

At least Clarke had the satisfaction of seeing millionaire gangster Fleetwood busted for illegal gun dealing.

```
Surveillance  Transcript:  016-26351  Location  ref:
FARM-1623
--------------------------------------------------------------
Joe  Clarke  (to  Mackey):  Looks  like  I  taught  you  my
last  lesson.  Don't  wind  up  like  me.
```

Emma Prince

Herself once a battered woman, Emma now runs a shelter for same. She was operating the shelter that was invaded by batterer Mike Holden, who slew six women, including his wife. Emma wa off premises at the time; thus she escaped the slaughter.

Mackey took an interest, pulling strings to find Emma a city building where she could establish a new shelter. He also dropped off some groceries. A strong attraction was developing between Mackey and Emma.

An abused woman lived across the street from Mackey's motel room. He could hear her screaming at night when her boyfriend was beating her up. He brought her to the Barn and put her together with Emma, who tried to convince the victim to break with her abuser and go to the shelter, if only for one night.

The battering boy-friend was present and lunged at Emma, who pushed him off the second-floor balcony. He was taken out of the station on a stretcher.

It was a clear-cut case of self-defense, but sometimes regulations have to be followed, even in a police station. Emma was charged with assault and bailed out by Mackey.

Their first amorous encounter did not end well.

Another time when Emma and Mackey were together, Corrine Mackey came to his motel room to confront him about the divorce papers he'd served her with.

She didn't see Emma, but she saw enough to know that Vic had a woman in the room.

Coyote Jack

Mexican-American Jack is a coyote, that is, a people smuggler who transports illegal immigrants across the U.S.-Mexico border for a fee.

Ninety-nine out of a hundred times, the traffic runs north, from Mexico to the United States. However, every now and then, someone wants to reverse direction, to be smuggled out of the United States into Mexico.

Vendrell gives Coyote Jack a warm north-of-the-border welcome.

Such persons are almost always fugitives.

It is known that Vic Mackey and Shane Vendrell were in contact with Coyote Jack on the day that Gilroy slipped his tails from the D.A.'s office and vanished.

It's possible that Coyote Jack smuggled Gilroy across the border into Mexico.

10. THE INSIDE LINE

An investigation is like a vacuum cleaner: it picks up a lot of dirt. Much of it is worthless and has to be thrown away. Sometimes, though, some valuable nuggets of intelligence turn up in the dustheap.

People will say things in private (especially when they don't know they're talking to an undercover investigator) that they'd never admit to in a court of law.

Information, disinformation, rumors, half-truths, suspicions, offhand remarks, and popular sentiment all make up part of the background noise of data, from which must be sifted the grains of intelligence.

Intelligence is not fact, but it is worth noting.

What follows is a survey of what might be called the Farmington Inside Line: the insider's take on some of the precinct's abiding mysteries.

Urban legends? Conspiracy theories? The naked truth?

You decide.

177

Lionel Phipps

Mackey put the squeeze on Rondell Robinson. He told Rondell that, if he didn't roll on his boss Phipps, he'd plant Rondell with drugs and bust him instead. Mackey gave Connie the hooker a bag of crack cocaine. Crack cocaine draws a stiffer sentence than possession of powder cocaine. Connie planted the drugs, hiding them in the bathroom.

Knowing that the drugs were in place, Mackey brought Rondell to Aceveda. Rondell swore that Phipps had crack coke at his place. Aceveda got a search warrant, the cops found the planted drugs (and the guns that had been used for a drive-by shooting), Phipps was busted, and the newly formed Strike Team had its first big win.

Terry Crowley

Aceveda wasn't shy about trying to nail Vic Mackey. Detectives Wagenbach and Wyms, investigators from IAD, and others were privy to some of his ideas on the subject of Mackey and the Strike Team.

Here's how Aceveda thought the killing of Terry Crowley went down: Crowley agreed to work undercover against Mackey.

IAD Surveillance Photo: #33.
Subject: Crowley funeral.

He knew that, if he helped take down even a dirty cop, he'd be through in the department. He wanted a guarantee that he'd have a career after testifying. He wanted the Justice Department to guarantee him a good job in Washington, D.C.

Aceveda agreed to arrange this through his longtime friend Moses Hernandez, who worked in the DOJ's L.A. office. Hernandez had to go through his superior, who called Assistant Chief Gilroy for clarification. Gilroy tipped Mackey that Crowley was working against him.

Mackey did the rest, turning the raid against drug dealer Two-Time into a death trap for Crowley.

Two-Time's girlfriend was present at the time of the raid. However, she fled to one part of the house, while Two-Time raced to the bathroom with a gun in one hand and a bag of drugs in the other. She didn't see the actual shooting. She stated that she heard a volley of shots, then a pause, then a single shot ten to fifteen seconds later.

Seizing on that, Aceveda put together a theory of what happened. The first volley was the gunfire exchanged between the Strike Team and Two-Time. Bullets from that volley killed Two-Time. The pause that followed was occasioned by one of the squad securing Two-Time's gun and turning it on Terry Crowley.

IAD Surveillance Photo: #29. Subject: Two-Time's funeral.

Two shots were fired at Crowley, one hitting him in the face and wounding him fatally. The murder being committed with Two-Time's gun, all that remained was to hang the kill on him. He was dead and therefore unable to contradict the frame-up.

This was the theory Aceveda was working on when he called on Dutch Wagenbach to help him grill Shane Vendrell for a grueling ninety-minute session.

Vendrell never cracked, but he became increasingly flustered and nervous, until Mackey showed up, ending the session.

Ara's Pastry Raid

During the drug bust at Ara's Pastry Shop and Bakery (a front for the Armenian mob), six bricks of cocaine and a large cache of drug-buy cash were found. Mackey and Vendrell stole the money and two bricks of cocaine.

That night, Vendrell stopped off to visit Amy, one of his girlfriends. He left the drugs hidden in the department-issue blue Navigator SUV he was driving that day. While he was inside, the vehicle was stolen. He went looking for it in

Amy's car. Seeing a blue Navigator SUV, he pulled it over at gunpoint. It was the wrong vehicle.

Learning of the incident, Aceveda put out an APB on the Navigator. The vehicle was spotted by Patrol Unit 1-Tango-13, Officers Danny Sofer and Julien Lowe. Aceveda got to the SUV before Mackey could.

There were no drugs in the vehicle. Deena Klein, the car thief, told Aceveda that there had been two bricks of cocaine in the Navigator and that she'd passed them to her boyfriend. Aceveda went to the boyfriend's residence but found Mackey had gotten there first.

The boyfriend was found dead of a cocaine overdose, but no drugs were found. Aceveda figured that Mackey had found them and moved them out before he'd arrived.

Julien Lowe had indeed seen Mackey and Vendrell steal the drugs. However, Mackey used the threat of outing Julien as gay to get him to back off on the statement he'd filed with IAD. With Julien disavowing the statement, the drug theft case against Mackey was dead.

The cocaine was later passed to Rondell Robinson, Mackey's protected drug partner, with the Strike Team claiming the lion's share of the resale profits.

Connie's Dead John

Hooker Connie Riesler was attacked by a john with a knife who slashed her badly around the neck and shoulders. She escaped, but the wound left a bad scar. The john was later arrested and convicted.

After the attack, Connie started carrying a gun in her purse when she went out tricking. She was also a heavy user of crack cocaine, which accelerates mental and emotional instability—to say the least.

When the Streetwalker Strangler's fifth victim was found, Connie's mental equilibrium was further destabilized. After a john got rough, she thought he was the serial killer. Panicking, she grabbed her gun and shot him dead.

He wasn't a serial killer. He was an insurance salesman from Fresno who'd gotten rough. Now she was stuck in a cheap motel room with a dead body.

She contacted Mackey. He went to her and cooked up a cover story. The john had been beating her; she'd gotten hold of the gun and shot him in self-defense.

One trouble: she hadn't been beaten.

To buttress the story with credible physical evidence, Mackey gave her a beating. She told her story to arresting officers and stuck with it. The cover story held, and no charges were filed.

Wrong Man Raid

```
Surveillance  Transcript:  044-21481  Location  ref:
FARM-3215
------------------------------------------------------------
Mackey: We made this mess. We're gonna clean it up.
```

Mackey and Lemansky screwed up. When Chaco Orozco fled, he looked like he was reaching for something. Thinking it was a gun, Lemansky fired, downing him.

It wasn't a gun. It was a carton of cigarettes.

All streetwise cops carry a "throw-down" or "throwaway" gun with them on duty: a weapon with no history. If they wind up shooting an unarmed person, they plant the throwaway gun on them and claim it belonged to the suspect. It

saves a lot of problems in the long run.

Not this time. Mackey planted Chaco with a throwaway gun. Later, he learned that he and Lemansky had framed the wrong man. Chaco was trying to quit the gang life. He was clean of any involvement with Los Mags, Hector Estanza's truckjacking crew. His sister, Tigre, had broken up with Estanza and Chaco had been protecting her.

Now, with Chaco in the hospital, Lemansky took over guarding Tigre. Complicating the picture even more, he found himself attracted to her.

To make things right, Mackey and Lemansky tried to steal "Chaco's" gun from the Barn evidence room but were unable to do so.

When the gun was being shipped from the Barn to Central in a police delivery van, Mackey and the Strike Team struck. They disguised themselves as Estanza's truckjacking crew. This wasn't hard to do, since the robbers always wore masks.

Estanza bore some distinctive tattoos, including one of a winged snake on his forearm. It was a popular tatt with Los Mags bangers. Mackey had a skin artist draw a wash-off tattoo on his arm in the same place Estanza had his. He made sure that the driver of the police delivery van had plenty of opportunities to get a good look at that tattoo during the hijacking.

The others broke into the van, stealing only the throwaway Chaco gun. Before leaving, they tagged the van with spray-painted Los Mags graffiti and shot out the tires. They used an untraceable stolen car for the hijacking.

Based on the driver's identification, an arrest warrant was issued for Estanza and his crew. The arrest was made by the Strike Team. Mackey planted Estanza with the gun used to shoot out the police van's tires.

Ballistics confirmed that this was the gun used in the hijacking, solidifying the case against Estanza. He and his crew were jailed.

With the throwaway gun stolen, there was no case against Chaco Orozco, and all charges were dropped.

Aceveda Rape Allegations

La Unidad reporter Tereza Varela got a story from Maureen Wilmore, daughter of influential publisher Chester Wilmore. Maureen Wilmore said that, when she and Aceveda were college students, he'd raped her. Before Varela could publish the charges, Aceveda's campaign manager, Jorge Machado, pulled some strings and got Varela fired.

She went freelance, continuing to shop her story around to various news outlets.

During this period, Aceveda visited Maureen Wilmore two times, trying to persuade her to drop her story. The second time, Wilmore was wired with a recording device that Varela had given her. She tried to entrap Aceveda into making incriminating remarks confirming her story.

Discovering the recorder, Aceveda took it from her. He told her that they both knew her story was untrue, that he hadn't raped her. Rather than harassing her, she'd harassed him, stalking him and ultimately attacking him with a penknife.

She retorted that she had been raped in college, by two friends of his. They'd picked up on a remark of his that she liked to be tied up for kinky sex. They went to her dorm room, bound her, and raped her.

Aceveda, shocked, said that he'd never known that.

Wilmore's admission was caught on tape, on the recorder. It is believed that Aceveda kept the tape. In any case, following this encounter, Wilmore repudiated her original accusations and instructed her attorney to break off all contact with Varela.

Aceveda remained composed despite the rape allegation.

Rondell and Tio

Mackey was in partnership with drug dealer Rondell Robinson. In exchange for a hefty share of the profits, Mackey let Rondell sell drugs in the district. When Rondell's own drug use made him unreliable, his lieutenant, Tio, approached Mackey, trying to sell him on a regime change.

Mackey gave the okay. Tio had Rondell hit and took his place as the Farm's protected drug dealer.

Gilroy: Red Pavement

On top of everything else, Assistant Chief Ben Gilroy was a drunk. He was drunk on the night he was driving a blue Mercedes with a female passenger and accidentally struck and killed Anthony Nunez and kept on going. He called on Mackey for help, citing their long friendship.

The problem was that there was a witness. Nunez was a Toros gang member, as was his pal Jesus Rosales. They'd been out on the corner selling drugs when Gilroy had struck Nunez. Rosales had seen Gilroy—and his female friend.

The hit-and-run case was assigned to Dutch Wagenbach. That meant Mackey had to work harder. Dutch was smart.

Mackey pitched the hit-and-run as a gang killing, a toss and shoot where the gang members throw the victim in the path of an oncoming vehicle, then fire their guns to chase the driver away, leaving the kill to look like a hit-and-run accident.

Dutch wasn't buying. He discovered that the female passenger in the car was Sedona Tellez, who'd vanished around the time of the accident.

Mackey got hold of Jesus Rosales, the witness in the case. He offered a deal. If Rosales would keep quiet about what really happened, he'd have a friend in the department—Mackey.

But Ben Gilroy crossed Mackey. He shot Rosales dead. Mackey was pissed, but there was nothing for him to do but continue with the cover-up. He and Gilroy dumped the body in Los Mags territory, to make it look like a gang killing.

That drove a wedge between Mackey and Gilroy. Mackey kept looking for Sedona Tellez, even after Gilroy warned him not to.

Gilroy turned up the heat. He went to Mackey's house, where he was welcomed inside by Corrine Mackey. She believed his story about Vic's having invited him over for dinner. Vic was so busy at work, it would be just like him to forget something like that, she thought. She and Gilroy had a nice pleasant visit.

Gilroy called Mackey and let him know where he was. Mackey freaked. A Sheriff's Office substation was located near the Mackey house. They could get there quicker than he could. He called them up and told them to send some deputies to his house. When they got there, Gilroy had already left, leaving a bewildered Corrine Mackey to wonder what all the fuss was.

Mackey didn't tell her. He moved his family out of the house and into a safely anonymous motel, where they were guarded by Lemansky.

Mackey moved hard against Gilroy. He put Aceveda on the paper trail of Gilroy's twisted financial dealings. Aceveda
unraveled the details of Gilroy's illegal real estate scam.

Gilroy was making moves of his own. He told Aceveda to get out a search warrant for Mackey's house. Aceveda held off on getting the warrant. Learning of it, Mackey figured that Gilroy had planted him with something when he'd last been at the Mackey house.

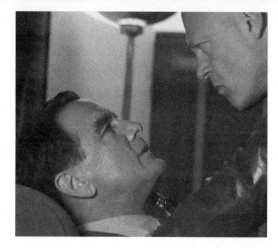

He and his men tore apart the house until they found what they were looking for: the gun that Gilroy had used to kill Jesus Rosales.

By wiping it clean of his fingerprints and planting it in the house, he'd hoped to tag Mackey for the kill.

Dutch Wagenbach found Sedona Tellez, and Aceveda got to her to flip against Gilroy. Mackey and Vendrell found Gilroy and busted him instead of liquidating him. Corrine Mackey went home, discovering that the house had been trashed. She didn't know it was the result of the frantic search for the gun. If she had, it probably would've made things worse.

She packed up the kids and walked out on Mackey.

```
Surveillance   Transcript:   021-37654   Location   ref:
FARM-1744
---------------------------------------------------------------
Gilroy: Vic, we were friends.

Mackey: You were the one who threatened my family.
```

Navaro Quintero

While Mackey was preoccupied with finding his missing wife and kids, Shane Vendrell invested a big chunk of Strike Team loot in a shipment of cocaine supplied by Customs Officer Jasper, one of Mackey's regular sources for drugs.

Jasper had gotten the drugs in Mexico, from major trafficker Navaro Quintero. When the shipment reached Farmington and drug dealer Tio, it was discovered that the entire load was poisoned.

It was a ploy by the brothers, Navaro and Armadillo Quintero, to destabilize competing drug dealers in the Farm, where Armadillo was busy setting up operations. Mackey, Vendrell, Lemansky, and Gardocki went to Tijuana, to see about a refund.

While trying to buy guns, Vendrell was robbed and had his badge stolen. This was the badge that later turned up on the black market to be bought by Hrach, one of Alex Eznik's mob.

The Strike Team abducted Navaro, holding him for a $400,000 ransom. His men paid the money, but Mackey crossed them, keeping both the money and Navaro.

Knocking Navaro out with drugs, they locked him in their car trunk and drove him back across the border into the United States, where he was turned over to federal authorities and imprisoned.

Armadillo Quintero

Armadillo Quintero was weeding out the competition. He burned down Tio's house, and later Tio.

For payback, Mackey held Armadillo's face against a hot stovetop burner, searing his face and scarring him. In hindsight, it would have been better for all concerned (except Armadillo himself) if Mackey had just put a bullet in the drug lord's brain.

Armadillo's counterpunch was not long in coming. He flooded the schools with heroin. He sent Mackey a message by having Ronnie Gardocki beaten and tortured, burning his face the same way Armadillo's had been burned by Mackey.

For the Strike Team, Armadillo was too dangerous to live. There was no way they were going to bring him in alive, to testify about his twisted duel with the Barn's rogue cops.

As they were closing in, Armadillo saw them coming and wisely surrendered to other Barn cops instead.

Mackey has nothing to declare.

Armadillo told Mackey that if the charges weren't dropped so he could walk, he'd tell all. Mackey wasn't going to let him off the hook. He told Vendrell and Lemansky that he was prepared to give himself up and take all the heat. He'd keep them out of it.

Vendrell and Lemansky took action of their own. A ready instrument lay near at hand in the form of Pinto. Pinto was an old-school Farmington banger who'd been pushed to the sidelines by Armadillo's Mexican-born clique.

Vendrell and Lemansky sought him out and cut a deal. If Pinto performed properly, they'd see that his aged mother was financially taken care of while he was behind bars.

Pinto needed little encouragement. Since Armadillo's advent, Pinto had gone into eclipse and was neither respected nor feared. He had something to prove.

First, he got himself arrested. He did so by walking down the sidewalk in broad daylight, smoking a marijuana joint and blowing smoke in Officer Danny Sofer's face. She apprehended him and brought him to the Barn. She searched him thoroughly before locking him in a holding cell.

While he was in there, someone, most likely Vendrell or Lemansky, passed him a knife. Pinto used it to stab Armadillo to death. Pinto was once more a respected man, a killer. The prestige would serve him well on his return to prison.

With Armadillo dead, Mackey—and the rest of the squad—were home free.

Gilroy: Over and Out

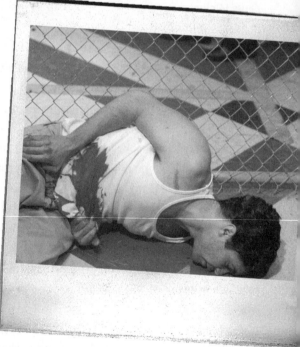

Civilian Auditor Lanie Kellis teamed with the D.A. to use Gilroy against Mackey. Gilroy was under house arrest, awaiting trial. He contacted Mackey, saying he was on the run and needed help to flee to Mexico. Once he got there, he would take a plane to extradition-free Brazil.

Sedona Tellez had gotten almost all of their money, but he still had some $70,000 stashed away. With the help of Mackey and Vendrell, the money was recovered.

Gilroy was drinking heavily at the time. He tried to rope Mackey into admitting he'd killed Terry Crowley. Mackey, suspicious, found a small tape recorder that Gilroy had hidden on his person. He discovered that Gilroy had been tailed, that a couple of detectives were watching the apartment where he'd hidden Gilroy.

Mackey went forward with the plan, adding some new twists.

He got Gilroy partially sobered up and told him there was still a way to make this a win-win situation. He'd arrange to have Gilroy smuggled out of the country into Mexico. But Gilroy had to do his part. He had to lose the detectives shadowing him and carry out an errand.

Gilroy was given $10,000 of his own money to pay the coyotero (people smuggler) in advance. He managed to shake his tail and meet the connection. He handed an envelope with the money in it to a man he thought was the coyotero.

Later, he rendezvoused with Mackey and Vendrell. Mackey told him that he'd taken out an insurance policy. He'd hired a hit man to kill Gilroy if he ever showed his face in this country again.

Or rather, Gilroy had hired the hit man—with his own money. The man Gilroy had met and handed the money envelope to was not a people smuggler—he was a contract killer.

The $10,000 was payment on a contract to kill Gilroy if Mackey should ever give the word. All he had to do was make a phone call to set the murder man in motion. The hit man had gotten a good look at Gilroy's face.

Mackey and Gilroy went way back. They'd been friends. To protect against going soft, Mackey gave the killer's phone number to Vendrell. Vendrell had no feeling for Gilroy and would just as soon see him dead as not.

Gilroy was given $60,000—his $70,000, less the $10,000 that had been paid to the hitter. Coyote Jack was on hand, in his pickup truck. Mackey had arranged for Jack to smuggle Gilroy into Mexico. Gilroy got in the pickup and it drove away.

Money Train

The Armenian mob had a money-laundering drop site somewhere in Farmington. Money from the mob's West Coast operations was funneled to the site. There the cash was packaged and loaded aboard an outward-bound ship, for delivery to a destination where it could be laundered.

The operation was called the Money Train, since illicit cash from up and down the coast was trucked into the site. The original site was at 9201 Escovida.

After the arrest of mob boss Alex Eznik, the site was changed. The new locale was somewhere in the industrial belt, a wasteland of warehouses, loading docks, and abandoned factories.

Within a day or two of the primary election, on a night in early April, the new drop site was hit. What happened that night is unclear; the initial reports are vague, fragmentary.

This much is known:

The process was almost done. In a day or two, the collected funds would be loaded aboard ship. On this night, some of the gang's enforcers caught two of the money loaders trying to steal some money. They made them lie down and slew them execution-style on the spot. The rest of the workers were unharmed and kept on loading the cash.

Suddenly, a gang of four ski-masked bandits armed with assault rifles appeared. They stole the money, loading it in a van and driving away.

With them they took one man from the drop site, Dach, a mobster who'd been shot, not fatally. It's suspected that he was the inside man on the heist, the finger man who'd set up the robbery with some outside confederates.

Dach was dropped off at a clinic. As soon as he was patched up, he fled. Mobsters searching his abandoned house found a bagful of the stolen money. One may be sure that they're looking very hard for Dach.

Found near the drop site was a dump truck that had been reported stolen the night before the heist. The company had a contract to pick up trash at the warehouse that was doubling as the drop site.

Shortly before the robbery, the garbage truck arrived as part of its normal routine. The drop site guards didn't know the hijacked truck was in unfriendly hands. The gates were opened; the truck entered the yard, emptied out the Dumpsters, and drove away. It's believed that it served as some kind of Trojan horse, allowing the bandits to be smuggled inside the fence.

This increases the likelihood that the robbery was an inside job.

It would all be listed as one more spectacular unsolved crime, except for a slight detail. It may be only coincidence; it may be something more.

A few weeks before the Money Train heist, Vic Mackey and Shane Vendrell were observed meeting with Leith, a high-end real estate broker.

Leith specializes in big-money real estate investments in developing properties, multimillion-dollar deals that are stratospherically beyond the reach of a cop's savings.

Using real estate investments to launder dirty money is a well-known ploy. Leith has a clean record of apparently handling only legitimate investments. However, it's known that he handled the sale on the building bought by drug dealer Tio, Mackey's now-deceased associate.

Subject: Money Train Case. SENSITIVE--INFORMANT PHOTO.

The implication is that perhaps Mackey and Vendrell were anticipating coming into a large sum of cash that they were looking to park in a safe, legal investment. Of course, this is pure speculation, based on the slim fact of their meeting with Leith a few weeks before the heist.

Still, it may be worth noting that the rip-off was pulled by four masked bandits.

The Strike Team has four members. It would be interesting to know what Mackey and company were doing on the night of the heist.

No doubt, they'll all have airtight alibis.

```
Surveillance  Transcript:  029-72621  Location  ref:
FARM-6292
-----------------------------------------------------------------
Mackey: When  we  retire,  we're  going  to  play  golf
together every day.

Vendrell: I never played.

Mackey: I'll teach you.

Vendrell: I'd really like that.
```

Late-breaking Developments

On primary election day, Vic Mackey went to police headquarters for a meeting behind closed doors with Chief Bankston.

When he emerged, he had the chief's endorsement for his continuing to remain as the leader of the Farmington Division Strike Team.

EPISODE GUIDE

Season 1

Episode 1: Pilot

Written by Shawn Ryan
Directed by Clark Johnson
Airdate: 3/12/02

Captain Aceveda suspects that Strike Team leader Detective Vic Mackey is in collusion with favored district drug dealers. Aceveda makes a deal with new team member Terry Crowley to work undercover to get enough on Mackey for a conviction.

Detectives Claudette Wyms and Dutch Wagenbach investigate the murder of Nancy Reborg, slain by her crackhead ex-husband, who then sold their eight-year-old daughter, Jenny, to a sex deviate. When their prime suspect, sadistic pedophile Dr. Grady, refuses to talk, Aceveda turns him over to Mackey to find the location of the missing girl.

Later, during a night raid by the Strike Team against drug dealer Two-Time, Terry Crowley is mortally wounded—and the viewer is forced to confront the naked truth about Vic Mackey.

Episode 2: Our Gang

Written by Shawn Ryan
Directed by Gary Fleder
Airdate: 3/19/02

Terry Crowley gets a hero's funeral, while both Internal Affairs Division (IAD) and Aceveda launch their own investigations into his death. IAD finds that Crowley was killed in the line of duty by Two-Time, while Aceveda believes—but can't prove—that Mackey was the killer. Claudette and Dutch probe the shooting of a food vendor and learn that he was shot for refusing to pay protection to the Los Mags street gang. The shooter is baby banger Olman, a young teen who pulled the trigger to gain entrance to the gang and whose painful initiation rite is interrupted by the Strike Team.

Episode 3: The Spread

Written by Glen Mazzara
Directed by Clark Johnson
Airdate: 3/26/02

It's sweeps day at the Barn, which means that the precinct officers are busy serving outstanding warrants. A routine arrest leads Mackey to apprehend NBA superstar Derrick Tripp, whose team is in town to play an important game against the Lakers. Mackey, a big Lakers fan, holds Tripp incommunicado at a private apartment for hours, as game time nears.

Connie, Vic's street hooker informant, is slashed by a violent "john," leading Dutch Wagenbach to theorize that the assailant is a serial killer who's been slaying street prositittutes and posing them facedown.

Episode 4: Dawg Days

Written by Kevin Arkadie
Directed by Stephen Gyllenhaal
Airdate: 4/2/02

Detective Curtis "Lemonhead" Lemansky and Officer Danny Sofer are moonlighting, working as private security at a party at the Shake Club to celebrate the upcoming release of an album by hip-hop recording artist Tyesha. Once the discovery and girlfriend of producer T-Bonz, she's now the protégé and girlfriend of producer Kern Little. Both T-Bonz and Little are involved in district drug dealing, too. The animosity between the two flares up at the club, resulting in a shooting that leaves four dead.

Courting favor with political kingmaker Jorge Machado, David Aceveda sets Claudette and Dutch in search of a missing migrant worker who's married to Machado's maid.

Mackey shuttles between T-Bonz and Little, trying to head off a gang war. When neither proves amenable to reason, he puts them both together in a confrontation from which only one can emerge alive.

Episode 5: Blowback

Written by Kurt Sutter
Directed by Clark Johnson
Airdate: 4/9/02

A bakery that's a front for an Armenian drug mob is raided by the Strike Team and backup units. Officer Julien Lowe sees Mackey and Shane Vendrell steal two bricks of coke from the drug stash. Julien tells Aceveda what he's seen.

Shane visits a girlfriend at her place, only to learn that his department-issued SUV with the drugs inside it has been stolen. Aceveda gets wind of the theft and races with Mackey to see who'll find the vehicle and its load of incriminating evidence first.

Episode 6: Cherrypoppers

Written by Scott Rosenbaum
Directed by Clark Johnson
Airdate: 4/16/02

A teenage hooker is the fifth victim of the Streetwalker Strangler, a serial slayer who's been preying on district prostitutes. For an intensive twenty-four-hour effort, Dutch Wagenbach takes command of an all-precinct operation to find the killer. Vic Mackey's part of the investigation leads him to the discovery of a sex club vice ring specializing in underage teenage girls.

Unnerved by her recent slashing, Connie mistakes a violent john for the Streetwalker Strangler and shoots him dead, then calls on Mackey for help.

The real serial killer, however, remains unknown and at large.

Episode 7: Pay in Pain

Written by Shawn Ryan
Directed by D. J. Caruso
Airdate: 4/23/02

A mass murderer runs wild at a gun club/target range frequented by members of the Toros street gang, killing eight. One of the victims is the gang leader's pregnant girlfriend. Vic Mackey teams with a gang expert from another district to track the killer. What looked like a gang-related massacre begins to take on a different aspect when the killer strikes again, this time at a neighborhood grocery store.

Aceveda passes along Julien's sworn statement to Internal Affairs, which opens an investigation into the alleged Strike Team drug theft. Julien's action in making the charges opens a rift between him and his partner and training officer Danny Sofer.

Assistant Chief Gilroy attempts to cool the red-hot Aceveda/Mackey feud.

Episode 8: Cupid & Psycho

Written by Glen Mazzara
Directed by Guy Ferland
Airdate: 4/30/03

When details of the supposedly confidential Internal Affairs probe become front-page news, Gilroy accuses Aceveda of leaking the story. Aceveda reassigns the Strike Team members to different partners. Mackey teams with Claudette Wyms to find a stash of brain-burning "crank," while Shane Vendrell and Dutch tackle a year-old killing whose trail seems to have gone cold.

Julien's tangled private life offers Mackey a handle for getting the other to retract his drug-theft charges.

Episode 9: Throwaway

Written by Kevin Arkadie
Directed by Leslie Libman
Airdate: 5/7/02

Hunting a vicious crew of truck hijackers, Mackey and Lemansky mistakenly shoot former gang member Chaco Orozco and plant a gun on him. To their chagrin, they learn that not only was Chaco unarmed, but he's innocent, too. Guarding Chaco's sister, Tigre, Lemansky becomes strongly attracted to her, putting him on a collision course with her ex-boyfriend, Hector, the real leader of the truck hijackers. Lemonhead and Mackey move to set the situation right.

During a family visit, Claudette puts her daughter's fiancé into an interrogation room and grills him about his intentions.

Episode 10: Dragonchasers

Written by Scott Rosenbaum and Kurt Sutter
Directed by Nick Gomez
Airdate: 5/14/02

Working undercover to crack a bait-and-bash racket, Shane Vendrell rubs up against exotic dancer Tulips, who lures him into an alley, where he's attacked by her male accomplice.

A chance incident observed by Danny and Julien puts Dutch on the trail of Sean Taylor, who he suspects of being the Streetwalker Strangler. Dutch and the crafty, manipulative Taylor engage in a battle of wits and wills to see who'll crack first.

Drug-addicted street hooker Connie tries to get straight, while Danny is bitten by an HIV-positive male prostitute.

Episode 11: Carnivores

Story by James Manos, Jr.
Teleplay by Kevin Arkadie and Glen Mazzara
Directed by Scott Brazil
Airdate: 5/21/02

Vic's drug-dealing associate Rondell Robinson feuds with a local Nation of Islam (NOI) mosque. Violence escalates, causing NOI minister Xavier Salaam to lead a nonviolent but tension-fraught occupation of the Barn.

Claudette and Dutch hunt a trio of home invaders who've brutally victimized an elderly Korean-American couple.

Aceveda confronts his past and fights to save his political future as his long-ago college girlfriend surfaces to accuse him of rape.

Episode 12: Two Days Of Blood

Written by Kurt Sutter and Scott Rosenbaum
Directed by Guy Ferland
Airdate: 5/28/02

The district is rocked by the murders of two women who called the Barn's 911 emergency number, only to have police arrive at the scene an hour later, after they've been killed. Community unrest explodes into riots.

Assistant Chief Gilroy calls on his long friendship with Mackey to convince him to cooperate in covering up a hit-and-run killing. At the same time, Gilroy horns in on the precinct, attempting to make Aceveda the patsy for the fatal 911 delay and subsequent rioting.

Mackey and Aceveda must work together to save their own necks, but when Vic looks too closely into Gilroy's doings, Gilroy threatens his family.

Episode 13: Circles

Written by Shawn Ryan
Directed by Scott Brazil
Airdate: 6/4/02

A trio of shooters makes fake 911 calls to lure police into fatal ambushes. Mackey discovers that Gilroy has been undermanning police coverage in the neighborhood to create a crime wave and depress property values, with the object of making a killing in real estate speculation. While tracking down the 911 ambush killers, Vic is also on a collision course with Gilroy.

The chaos and uncertainty are too much for Vic's wife Corrine, who takes the kids and flees to parts unknown, leaving him to come home to an empty house.

Season 2

Episode 1: The Quick Fix

Written by Shawn Ryan and Glen Mazzara
Directed by Scott Brazil
Airdate: 1/7/03

Five weeks have passed since Corrine went away, and Vic's got a private detective looking for his family.

Shane Vendrell uses the team's stashed cash to buy a load of cocaine—which turns out to be poisoned. Behind it are the Quintero brothers, Mexican drug mobsters. Armadillo is in Farmington burning rival drug dealers to death, while Navaro is taking care of business in Tijuana. Vic and the rest of the team go south of the border, looking for payback. They abduct Navaro and offer to ransom him back to his gang for four hundred grand.

Episode 2: Dead Soldiers

Written by Kurt Sutter
Directed by John Badham
Airdate: 1/14/03

Armadillo moves against Tio, Mackey's drug dealer of choice, burning down a building he owns. Mackey's efforts to protect Tio provoke the suspicions of Claudette Wyms, who is also working the case.

With his political career on track, Aceveda has a stake in keeping Mackey's doings secret. Complicating the picture is the presence of Lanie Kellis, a civilian auditor appointed by the city council to keep an eye on the Barn.

A series of confrontations causes Danny Sofer to fatally shoot Arab-American Zayed Al-Thani, resulting in serious professional and personal woes.

Vic puts the heat on Armadillo—literally.

Episode 3: Partners

Written by Scott Rosenbaum
Directed by Guy Ferland
Airdate: 1/21/03

A face from the past resurfaces when Mackey is visited by his onetime partner and mentor, ex-cop Joe Clarke. Clarke's public beating of career criminal Fleetwood Walker resulted in Walker's successfully suing the city for more than a million dollars, and Clarke's loss of his job, pension, and ultimately, family.

Dutch works on Bob and Marcy Lindhoff, prime suspects in the disappearance and mutilation of a missing young woman. He psychologically hammers Marcy, thinking that if he can break her, he'll learn the truth about the case.

Clarke and Mackey interrupt Fleetwood in the middle of an illegal gun deal, triggering a wild shootout.

Episode 4: Carte Blanche

Written by Reed Steiner
Directed by Peter Horton
Airdate: 1/28/03

A badge stolen from Shane Vendrell in Mexico returns to feature in a Farmington jewelry shop homicide. The trail leads to Alex Eznik, top boss of the L.A. branch of the Armenian mob. Shane and Mackey go undercover, "pretending" to be crooked cops to get themselves into Eznik's confidence.

Claudette Wyms gets a second chance to try to nail Manny Sandoval, who dealt his way out of jail in the Cupid methedrine case.

The Strike Team learns of the Money Train, an Armenian mob money-laundering site hidden somewhere in the district.

Episode 5: Greenlit

Written by Kim Clements
Directed by Terrence O'Hara
Airdate: 2/4/03

Armadillo strikes again, unleashing a heroin epidemic targeted at teens and schoolchildren. The pressure's on Aceveda, whose election prospects are imperiled.

Connie makes it official by becoming Mackey's registered and contracted Confidential Informant.

Mackey tries to get to Armadillo by threatening to "greenlight" Navaro—that is, arrange to have him killed in prison. Armadillo has his own notions of family obligations, and counters by ordering the murder of every squad member.

Now the Strike Team has been threatened.

Episode 6: Homewrecker

Written by Shawn Ryan and Glen Mazzara
Directed by Scott Brazil
Airdate: 2/11/03

A massacre at a battered women's shelter leaves six women dead. Their slayer is Mike Holden, who killed his wife and every other adult female on the premises, then took away his four-year-old son.

Shelter manager and survivor Emma Prince piques Vic Mackey's interest in more ways than one.

Piquing Connie's interest is a $5,000 reward posted for information leading to the arrest of Mike Holden. Knowing of his obsessive interest in hookers, she arranges to be with him in his motel room, leading to a lethal hostage-taking situation.

Episode 7: Barnstormers

Written by Scott Rosenbaum
Directed by Scott Winant
Airdate: 2/18/03

His confidence shaken by the Bob and Marcy debacle, Dutch throws himself into a new rape-murder case.

Ronnie Gardocki confides in the other team members that he thinks he's being followed. This fails to stop them from proceeding with plans for a Money Train heist.

Emma Prince tangles with a batterer at the Barn, and later goes home with Vic. But their liaison is cut short before it begins by a ghastly surprise.

Episode 8: Scar Tissue

Written by Kurt Sutter
Directed by Paris Barclay
Airdate: 2/25/03

The torture-burning of Ronnie Gardocki has only intensified the squad's kill-or-be-killed struggle with Armadillo.

Corrine Mackey has a talk with Claudette in which she tells much but learns more.

With the Strike Team closing in, Armadillo saves his life by surrendering to other cops. Held at the Barn, he's a ticking time bomb. If he talks, the Strike Team members could wind up in jail. Vic decides to take all the blame himself to get the others off the hook. But Shane and Lemonhead have a plan to make things right.

Episode 9: Copilot

Written by Shawn Ryan and Glen Mazzara
Directed by Peter Horton
Airdate: 3/4/03

Forward into the past, with a flashback fourteen months earlier, to the Barn's opening day.

Detective Vic Mackey needs the job of Strike Team boss and persuades his friend and mentor, Assistant Chief Gilroy, to put him in the slot. Gilroy creates the Farmington Division and staffs it his way, except for the post of captain, which goes to ambitious, educated law enforcement professional David Aceveda.

Claudette and Dutch team up for the first time to tackle a kidnap ring.

With the pressure on to get results early, Vic and the rest of the team take a few shortcuts to bring gang boss Lionel Phipps to justice.

Episode 10: Coyotes

Written by Reed Steiner
Directed by Davis Guggenheim
Airdate: 3/11/03

Lanie Kellis locates the Barn's problems in the Aceveda/Mackey axis, but she can't prove it. Her scathing report on the precinct is leaked to the press, creating a public relations headache that reaches all the way up to the chief of police.

Ben Gilroy jumps bail, begging Vic to help get him out of the country and into Mexico. Mackey learns that Gilroy's playing a double game and makes some countermoves of his own.

Strike Team newcomer Tavon Garris shows he can play it rough or smooth when it comes to making a bust.

Episode 11: Inferno

Story by James Manos, Jr., and Kim Clements
Teleplay by Kim Clements
Directed by Brad Anderson
Airdate: 3/18/03

Negative publicity puts the Barn in a bad light, making it necessary to get a big win. Opportunity knocks in the form of Dante Fell, federally wanted fugitive and gangster who's returned home to the Farm for a visit. Mackey pumps Fell's old friend Kern Little for information, making him a lot of big promises he may not intend to keep.

Ronnie, released from the hospital and back at work, comes up with a plan to heist the Money Train.

A skeleton from Julien's closet reappears, one who won't take no for an answer.

Episode 12: Breakpoint

Written by Glen Mazzara
Directed by Felix Alcala
Airdate: 3/25/03

Where is Jeffrey Cole? The fourteen-year-old boy from a broken family was last seen on a street corner frequented by male hustlers, where he got into a car with an unknown man. Dutch thinks Jeffrey might have fallen victim to a serial killer with a proclivity for teen boys in tandem.

A pedophile named Adam is the leading suspect, and Mackey's not too particular about how he gets information from him.

The Barn's bad press sends Chief Bankston in search of Aceveda to deliver him an ultimatum.

Claudette Wyms reaches some final conclusions of her own and decides that the precinct needs a new boss: her.

Episode 13: Dominoes Falling

Written by Shawn Ryan
Directed by Scott Brazil
Airdate: 4/1/03

It's Primary Day, and Aceveda goes into the city council election several points behind. Should he lose, the loss of the precinct captaincy will soon follow.

Claudette's ex-husband is shot dead on the street by a stranger, and the only witness is her daughter Bonnie. Vic and Tavon terrorize gang leader Lops, discovering a diabolical gang murder plot to murder innocent citizens at random.

Shane, Lemonhead, and Ronnie are in place to make a move on the Money Train. But Vic's not there and time is fast running out.

Danny Sofer finds out her fate in the department, while Julien is savaged by a human rat pack.